Goodness Me it's Gluten Free

PASTA

By Vanessa Hudson

Copyright © 2014 Goodness Me Limited
Tauranga, New Zealand
www.goodnessme.co.nz
enquiries@goodnessme.co.nz

Published by: Goodness Me Limited
First edition: 2014

Design, Text, Photography:
All copyright © 2014 Vanessa Hudson

Copy Editor: Mary Hudson

Cover Photo: Pasta Making by Vanessa Hudson

ISBN: 978-0-473-28096-3

A CIP catalogue record for this book is available from the National Library of New Zealand.

The right of Vanessa Hudson to be identified as the author and photographer of this work in terms of section 96 of the Copyright Act 1994 is hereby asserted.

ACKNOWLEDGEMENTS

A huge thank you to my family and friends, you know who you are and although not named individually here in case I accidentally omit someone, each and every one of you are special to me in many different ways. Not least of which is all the support and encouragement you have each given me especially while writing this cookbook.

Not forgetting of course for some of you that meant eating countless pasta dishes, providing feedback and thankfully coming back willingly for more!

A special thanks to my friend Robbie Banks for taking the lovely photos of me in this cookbook.

Finally I want to express my appreciation to all of you who will use this cookbook, make the recipes and who then take the time to email me or post online your comments, questions and feedback. To hear that I have helped you find joy in eating gluten free makes the countless hours that go into writing cookbooks all worth it!

Grazie mille - thank you very much.

CONTENTS

INTRODUCTION

My appreciation for a diverse range of ingredients and cooking styles has been nurtured through extensive worldwide travel including many happy years spent living in Europe where the Mediterranean way of eating fast became one of my favourites. However, despite having had the pleasure of exploring Italy on three separate occasions I had never fully understood an Italian's passion for pasta until I made my first bowl of fresh homemade gluten free spaghetti. It curled around my fork like it was meant to and never had before. The sauce clung to and coated each strand like they were made for each other, which they were, instead of slipping and flicking everywhere like mass produced pasta does leaving the inevitable puddle of sauce in the bottom of the bowl. No this was different! Suddenly all the things I had heard said about pasta but never experienced were coming true, and then I took a bite. Wow!

Pasta it seems, outside of Italy, is so often just seen as a way of quickly filling hungry tummies that we rarely give it much thought, either in the preparation or as we shovel it laden with sauce into our mouths, but it doesn't have to be this way. I believe we should eat with intention, to stimulate the tastebuds and delight the senses, which is why I am so excited to be sharing with you the wide variety of recipes in this cookbook. There are of course still the very practical feed-the-family-fast recipes but without compromising on flavour and many recipes that are a little different from what you might expect - perfect for discerning tastebuds and entertaining.

Homemade egg pasta is full bodied, packed with protein and complex carbohydrates and with a lower GI index than mass produced pasta and other starchy carbohydrates - it's a true power food. I have embraced the Mediterranean way of using the freshest, best quality (not necessarily expensive) ingredients I can find and that is reflected in the recipes which often only incorporate a few key ingredients, thus letting each one truly shine and impart its unique flavour and texture to the dish.

I must confess though that I'm not Italian and don't have a nonna at my beck and call to teach me family pasta making secrets, but I can assure you this is not a prerequisite to being able to create delicious and satisfying homemade pasta. The recipes and techniques in this cookbook are proof of that, if I can do it I have every confidence you can too! All the pasta you see in the photos was handmade by me, in a home kitchen. The many varied handmade shapes you will find described within these pages might look a little different than the mass produced pasta you may be more familiar with, but I encourage you to embrace your creative spirit, give it a go and most of all have fun.

Along the way I hope you will fall as much in love as I have with the simplicity, diversity and extraordinary fresh flavour of the pasta and sauces in this cookbook.

Buon appetito!

GOODNESS ME PASTA BLEND

To make the gluten free pasta dough you will need some Goodness Me Pasta Blend flour. This blend uses predominantly whole grains ensuring it has a higher fibre and nutritional content, as well as being lower GI, than most commercially available blends. The gluten free flours used to make the Pasta Blend should be readily available at your local supermarket, bulk bin store, ethnic or whole foods market. It's a good idea to check the labels when buying each individual flour to make sure it has indeed been manufactured according to gluten free standards.

Makes 1.3kg (3lb)

300g (12oz) fine rice flour
400g (14oz) buckwheat flour
600g (1lb 5oz) fine maize flour

Ingredient Note:
Maize flour can be named or labelled in many different ways and can be made with maize or corn, but it is always **yellow.** The white maize cornflour commonly used for thickening sauces works differently in recipes because it is 100% starch, so please don't use it in the Goodness Me flour blends - you can see our website www.goodnessme.co.nz for more information about these flours. If you can't tolerate or don't want to use fine maize flour it can be successfully substituted for the same weight of sorghum flour.

Make the blend by thoroughly mixing together the flours so they are evenly combined.

The quantities at left, make much more than you need for a single batch of pasta but once made it stores well and can be used in a variety of cooking and baking applications. There are no preservatives in the blend, so the shelf life will be the same as labelled on the individual flours. The blend is best kept in a sealed storage container in a cool dry place.

The Pasta Blend is the same as the Baking Blend used in our *Goodness Me it's Gluten Free* Baking cookbook so you can use the Baking Blend for making the pasta dough if you have it.

CHOOSING THE RIGHT SIZE EGGS: The eggs you use are quite critical in gluten free pasta making so ensure your eggs are good quality, fresh and the correct size. In this comparison chart I have selected the sizes that most closely correspond to the two NZ egg sizes I have used in the recipes, always erring towards the heavier egg as a little more is better than not enough when making pasta. The weights given below are for the whole egg in its shell.

NZ	AUS	UK	USA	CA	EU
Jumbo Size 8	Jumbo	Very Large	Jumbo	Jumbo	Very Large
68g+	66.7–70g	73g+	71g/2.5oz+	70g	73g+
Standard Size 6	Large	Medium	Large	Large	Medium
53g+	50-58.2g	53-63g	57g/2oz+	56-62g	53-63g

IMPORTANT RECIPE NOTES

NEW ZEALAND STANDARD METRIC CULINARY MEASURES:

In all the recipes: 1 cup = 250ml, 1 Tablespoon = 15ml and 1 teaspoon = 5ml.

The pasta dough ingredients must be carefully measured but the sauces in this book should still give a similar result by using whatever the standard culinary cups and spoons are in your country, providing you use the same utensils throughout the recipe thus keeping the proportions the same. Culinary measuring cups and spoons are the sort used for baking, and not the spoons from your cutlery drawer as they are quite different in size.

OVENS:
In the recipes we use a fan bake/forced oven at the following temeratures **200°C** = 400°F = gas mark 6. **180°C** = 350°F = gas mark 4. **160°C** = 320°F = gas mark 2-3. All ovens are different so experiment to find out what is correct for your particular oven adjusting temperatures and time accordingly.

ABBREVIATIONS: *1 t = 1 teaspoon. 1 T = 1 Tablespoon. 1½ cups = 1 cup plus another ½ cup.*

ALLERGIES & INTOLERANCES:
The pasta dough and all the recipes are free from gluten, wheat, potato, soy and sesame and only two sauce recipes contain nuts.

The pasta dough is also dairy-free and many of the sauces are too, if you leave out the parmesan used for garnishing.

Always read the ingredients label of packaged items used in the sauces to ensure they are gluten free.

INGREDIENTS & SUBSTITUTIONS:
With so many sauces requiring so few ingredients it is worth making sure what you use is the freshest and best quality you can find, it really truly does make a difference to the finished dish. This does not always mean the most expensive ingredients, just quality; take the time to be selective.

Olive oil is used a lot in these recipes. Please do not substitute with another type of oil, this is especially important in the pasta dough where only olive oil will do. Besides it's good for you!

Another concession I have made in adapting traditional recipes to New Zealand ingredients it to substitute cream cheese for ricotta. If you can get quality ricotta by all means use it, cottage cheese is also a good substitute however if using either in place of cream cheese in the recipes you might also need to include an egg to get the "sticky" consistency required, especially when making filled pastas.

Where spinach is specified in a recipe it can be directly substituted for silverbeet or swiss chard, though do try to use the younger more tender leaves of these plants, and always remove the tough stalks before using.

Parmesan, oh what I would give for readily available and affordable parmesan in New Zealand. Yes you can find the real thing if you search for it here, but most of the easily sourced cheese called parmesan is sadly lacking in flavour compared to actual parmesan from Italy. I have often used a good strong extra tasty (mature) cheddar cheese instead of Parmesan in recipes like Lasagne as both a flavour and cost concession.

Canned or packaged goods vary slightly in size from country to country so use whatever is closest to the size specified in the recipe, it will not matter if there is a little more or a little less of the ingredient in the sauce.

EQUIPMENT:
Essential: A large stock pot, a large frying pan (a wok works well) big enough to hold the sauce and the pasta, a colander, a digital timer and a rolling pin.

Helpful: Pasta machine with spaghetti and fettuccine attachment, straight & fluted pasta wheels, pasta stirrer, long tongs, metal ruler, pasta brush, garganelli board and shaping pins, wooden work surface or chopping board.

BEFORE YOU BEGIN

In this cookbook I have focused on pasta shapes that you can make fresh in your own home with very little equipment.

One of the earliest references to the use of pasta in Italy is from 1154 in Sicily. However it seems that sheets of boiled dough may have been eaten in various cultures almost since the dawn of time. Pasta is now synonymous with Italy and can be found in a multitude of shapes and varieties, though no one seems to agree on just how many forms exist with numbers ranging from 300–600 depending on who you ask. To complicate things each region of Italy often has a different name for each shape (let alone the traditional regional sauces or fillings) with over 1300 names recorded throughout Italy.

Pasta making is not an exact science, it's all about feel and instinct, with climate and temperature playing a part in the dough making process. So with this in mind you may find it takes making a few batches of dough before you feel confident with your pasta making skills, remembering that adjustments will always need to be made with the changing seasons. That said relax and enjoy the process as making your own dough is exciting and satisfying - there's nothing quite like it.

Do measure the ingredients for the dough carefully as the proportions of flour to egg, oil and water are quite critical to getting a lovely workable dough. The protein and lecithin in eggs help with the elasticity and the olive oil gives pliability. Both essential in pasta made without wheat!

The sauces that accompany the pasta are however very forgiving so don't panic if you have a little more or a little less of something, just give it a go, you will probably still create a fabulous finished dish. Gli avanzi, leftovers are the backbone of traditional Italian peasant cooking so there are many sauce recipes in this cookbook where leftovers can be incorporated, and their use is encouraged. Think of it as culinary upcycling!

Pasta dough I feel is always best eaten fresh on the day it was made however if you want to keep it here are some guidelines: The pasta dough can be kept for a few days in the fridge tightly wrapped in plastic wrap, bring back to room temperature before using. The dough ball can also be frozen (and so can ravioli, see recipes for specifics) for up to a month as long as it's frozen in a well sealed bag and is thoroughly thawed before use, other pasta shapes are not recommended for freezing. You can also dry the pasta shapes by leaving to dry slowly away from drafts on a clean tea towel. Fettuccine and spaghetti are best dried initially hanging over something like a coat hanger, and then finished on a tea towel. Once the pasta has dried it should be stored at room temperature in an airtight container and is best used within the month though it will still be tasty long after that.

The size of pot, amount of water, salt and speed of boil are all important when cooking pasta. Use a large stock pot to cook the pasta as sufficient space is needed for the right quantity of water and to give the pasta space to move. A large pot with 4-5 litres of water can take up to 20 minutes to come to a rolling boil, longer than you might think. A rolling boil provides bubbles which aid the extra buoyant salted water to keep your pasta separated, moving around the pot and help it to cook evenly and perfectly. The water must be at a rolling boil (fast) before you start cooking the pasta – and yes the pasta will appear to roll in the water!

Don't overcook the pasta. Al dente is the Italian term literally meaning "to the tooth" used throughout the book and describes how the pasta should be cooked only until firm to the bite - not soft right through, as it will continue to cook slightly once removed from the water. So keep checking your pasta as it cooks. Fresh pasta cooks faster than dried, often in only 2-3 minutes.

TOP 20 PASTA TIPS & TRICKS

* Around 125g (4.5oz) fresh pasta is considered an adult main course serving.
* Pasta is best eaten fresh on the day it is made.
* Climate and temperature can change the way your pasta dough handles.
* To cook use a large stock pot, with water at a rolling boil (fast with bubbles).
* You will need about 1 litre (2pt) of water for every 100g (3.5oz) of pasta.
* Don't cook more than two batches of pasta at a time.
* The pasta water should be very salty and taste like the sea.
* For every 2 litres (4pt) of water add 1 heaped tablespoon of salt.
* Pasta does not need oil in the cooking water, it won't help and is a waste!
* Never put the lid on the pot once the pasta is in it.
* Stir the pasta when you put it in the pot to make sure it is all separated.
* Fresh pasta cooks fast, keep testing it and drain pasta when al dente.
* Always, always make the sauce wait for the pasta, not the other way round.
* Italians lubricate but don't suffocate their pasta with sauce, it's best that way.
* A few fresh, good quality (not necessarily expensive) ingredients go a long way.
* Don't let your pasta go naked; toss it in the sauce or olive oil before serving.
* Mixing the sauce evenly through the pasta is easier if you put the sauce on top.
* Soffritto is fantastic for adding both a flavour and a vegetable boost to sauces.
* With pasta as the base you can invent your own sauces, it's a fantastic fast food!

SOFFRITTO

Soffriggere is an Italian word meaning to cook at below frying temperature, fry slowly or under fried and so, as the name implies, the ingredients for soffritto are cooked in this way. In Italian cuisine, soffritto can often also be referred to as odori (smells that flavour the food), and in France is called mirepoix. It is typically prepared in a 2:1:1 ratio of onions, celery, and carrots. In most of Italy soffritto is gently sautéed in olive oil which releases the flavours to infuse any dish where soffritto is used. Garlic, fresh herbs and even pancetta make fabulous additions to a basic soffritto. When shopping in markets all over Italy greengrocers will ask if you would like odori or soffritto to go with your purchase as it is such a commonly used ingredient in Italian cuisine. I suggest you make it in bulk and freeze in smaller quantities. Then you will have this classic Italian "secret" ingredient ready on hand to add to any dish in seconds.

Makes 2-3 cups

2 medium onions
1 large celery stalk
1 good size carrot
1 T olive oil
Salt & pepper (to taste)

Parsley, oregano, basil, 2
  cloves garlic, 125g pancetta
  (all optional)

1. Dice all ingredients into the smallest dice possible (see photo). A blender/whizz can help with this or a mezzaluna (crescent shaped knife).
2. In a good sized frying pan add the oil, diced ingredients, salt and pepper.
3. Stir over a low heat until the onion is translucent and the vegetables are just tender around 5-7 minutes.
4. Remove from the heat, allow to cool down and then bag in ½ cup amounts. Soffritto can be frozen for several months.

Cook's Tip:
You can increase or decrease the quantities dependent on what you have on hand, always keeping the proportion of 2:1:1. Having bags of soffritto in the freezer will cut down on the preparation time for a lot of recipes, there is no need to defrost before use. It also adds extra nutrition to a meal, not to mention enhancing the flavour of red sauces, soups and stews!

GLUTEN FREE FRESH EGG PASTA

There are two recipes here to help you make the right amount of pasta for your family. Fresh pasta is I feel best eaten the day it is made though it can keep for several days in the refrigerator. The dough serving quantities below are a guide only as it really depends on appetite, and if you are making a main, side or lunch dish. An average adult main serve of pasta is between 100g-150g (3.5oz-5oz). For simplicity the sauce recipes suggest using either the full or half batch (which can also be a full batch divided in half if you prefer).

450g (1lb) full batch - serves 4

2 cups (300g/10.6oz) Pasta Blend
1 t xanthan gum (OR 2 t guar gum)
1 t salt
Pinch grated nutmeg (optional)
3 size 6 eggs
2 T (30ml) olive oil
4 T (60ml) water

185g (6.5oz) half batch - serves 2

¾ cup (115g/4oz) Pasta Blend
½ t xanthan gum (OR 1 t guar gum)
½ t salt
Pinch grated nutmeg (optional)
1 size 8 egg (note larger egg size)
1 T (15ml) olive oil
2 T (30ml) water
¼ cup extra Pasta Blend (if needed)

Ingredient Note:
Xanthan, guar gum and salt in these quantities are hard to weigh accurately so you will need to measure using a 5ml teaspoon.

Different climates and seasons affect the pasta making process changing the moisture content of the flour and therefore how much water is needed for the dough. Because of this the water is added gradually, later in the process.

1. Measure the water into a tiny bowl and set aside.
2. In another bowl carefully measure the Pasta Blend.
3. Add to the bowl the gum, nutmeg and salt. Whisk until evenly distributed through the Pasta Blend.
4. Tip the dry ingredients out onto a clean bench top and make a clear space in the middle of the flour (or keep making in the bowl if you prefer).
5. Into the clear space crack the egg(s) and add the olive oil. With a fork or small whisk beat the egg(s) and oil together.
6. Then slowly begin to stir and incorporate the flour into the egg. Keep doing this until most of the flour has combined and there is a messy dough mixture.
* **Recipe continues over page.**

Variation:
If you don't need gluten free pasta you can substitute the Pasta Blend for the same *weight* of "standard" or "type 00" flour and omit the gum.

The following steps will seem a little complicated and time consuming the first time you make pasta dough. But once you know what texture to look for and how the dough should feel, making pasta dough will become a lot faster and feel more natural, until you almost won't have to think about it.

7. With dry hands begin to pull together the remaining flour and dough until you have formed a messy ball. It can take a while for the dough to come together so do not rush it. Keep squishing and gathering for a couple of minutes, it will surprise you how much flour will become incorporated.

8. If you are having trouble getting all of the flour and dough bits incorporated, dip your fingers in the water bowl and with your wet fingers continue collecting up the flour and dough bits. Knead the water into the dough after each addition and repeat until everything is collected and incorporated and a tidy dough ball is formed.

9. Keep kneading by flattening the dough with the ball of your hand down and away from you, folding and turning to make sure all the ingredients (and any water) are well combined and that the texture is correct and uniform throughout. The texture of the dough will change as you knead the dough to become pliable and bendy. If that is not happening, gradually work in more water kneading as you go. After about five minutes there should be a soft ball of dough that can be easily kneaded, but that does not stick to the bench or your hand.

10. If the dough is a little sticky add a small dusting of flour until the right consistency is achieved.

11. To test if the dough is ready and the texture is correct depress the dough about 1cm (⅓") with your finger. The finger indent should have stretched the dough but not broken the surface. If the surface broke it is still a little dry, add a bit more water. If it still sticks to your finger then it is a little wet, add a bit more flour. Take note that it is better for the dough to end up slightly too wet than too dry. Each addition of water or flour should be thoroughly kneaded into the dough before assessing again if the texture is correct.

12. Cover the finished dough ball tightly with plastic wrap and rest on the bench for 30 minutes. The dough will relax during this time and become even softer. If it's very tacky to the touch after resting be a little more generous with the flour as the dough is rolled out for shaping.

Cook's Tip:
The dough is now ready to make into the pasta shape you require. However you can put the dough (still tightly covered) in the fridge at this stage if intending to shape your pasta much later on or the next day. But be sure to bring your dough up to room temperature again for about 30 minutes before using.

PASTA DOUGH THICKNESS GUIDE

Most types of pasta have an optimum thickness that the dough should be rolled out to and herein lies the challenge; how to give a thickness measurement that can be universally followed. I find trying to measure dough with a ruler to see if it is 2mm thick is totally impractical. With so many different pasta machines on the market, their varying thickness settings and also the option to hand roll pasta there needs to be a standardisation to make sure we can all achieve the same thickness of pasta dough. So when I recently heard about the simple guide explained below, I decided to implement it throughout this cookbook. I hope you will find it as easy to follow as I do. You will need a deck of standard playing cards for use with this guide.

HAND ROLLING

If you are hand rolling the pasta the best method I have found is to place two even stacks of cards on each side of your pasta dough e.g. 3 to a stack on each side for 3 card thickness then rest the rolling pin on top of the cards. If the rolling pin can sit on the cards without making an indent in the pasta you are at the right thickness, if not keep rolling until it can.

MACHINE ROLLING

If you have a pasta machine, I suggest you copy the simple table below and keep it with your machine as a quick reference guide.

The machine I currently use has settings from 7 (thickest) to 1 (thinnest). I measured the settings by seeing how many playing cards could freely pass through the rollers without turning the handle. Then I recorded the dial number on the machine that corresponded to the number of Card per Thickness in the middle column. This is what you should do with your machine adding your dial number to the My Pasta Machine column. The ones you will find referred to most in the recipes are in red. For example if the recipe says "roll out to 3 card thickness" then you would look at the chart and know you need dial setting no 3 (for example) on your pasta machine to achieve that thickness.

Goodness Me's Settings	Card per Thickness	My Pasta Machine
Dial No: 7	7 card: first stage for preparing the dough	Dial No:
Dial No: 6	6 card: rolling	Dial No:
Dial No: 5	5 card: rolling	Dial No:
Dial No: 4	4 card: used for some shaped and tubular pastas	Dial No:
Dial No: 3	3 card: most commonly used thickness	Dial No:
Dial No: 2	2 card: can be used for filled pasta e.g. ravioli	Dial No:
Dial No: 1	1 card: angel hair pasta – not often used	Dial No:

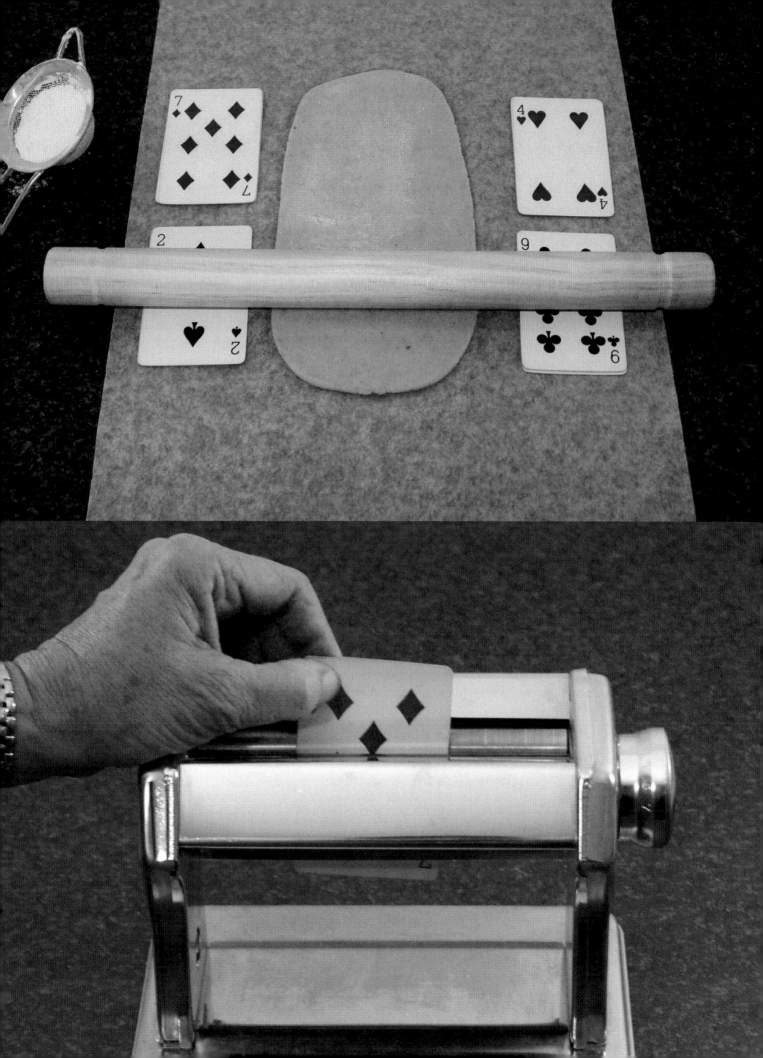

ROLLING OUT THE DOUGH

If the pasta shape being made requires a sheet of dough, follow these simple rolling out instructions.

BOTH: Begin by dividing the dough into even jumbo egg sized pieces. Take one piece while keeping the rest wrapped up to prevent drying out. Briefly knead the piece of dough in your hands to make it smooth and then flatten into a roughly oblong shape. I use baking paper for hand rolling on and also for resting dough sheets on as it means you will need to use less flour, making any offcuts easier to reuse and it also stops the dough from drying out too much; a side effect of using lots of flour.

HAND METHOD: Dust lightly with flour then begin to roll out on a piece of baking paper or a floured flat surface. I find it easiest to use baking paper making sure it's long enough to tuck between your tummy and the edge of the bench to give some resistance as you roll the pasta away from you. Only ever roll away from you not towards you, as it is more of a stretching motion rather than rolling. Place the rolled sheet of dough to one side on another piece of baking paper. Roll all the pieces of dough to the same stage making sure you cover the sheets with a clean tea towel to stop them drying out. In very hot weather, you might need to use a well wrung out dampened tea towel.

MACHINE METHOD: Dust dough lightly with flour and pass through the widest setting on your pasta machine. Fold the dough in thirds and roll again through the machine at the widest setting. Repeat at least three times until you have an oblong shaped piece of dough with fairly straight smooth lengthwise edges, after this step you no longer need to fold the dough. Place length of dough to one side on a piece of baking paper. Rolling all the pieces of dough to the same stage saves time. Make sure you cover up the sheets of dough with a clean tea towel to stop them drying out between rollings. In very hot weather, you might need to use a well wrung out dampened tea towel.
Repeat the rolling process (without folding) with each sheet of dough adjusting your machine one setting thinner each time until you reach the correct thickness on all the sheets for the type of pasta you are making. See the individual pasta shape recipes for the required thickness setting.

BOTH: Next trim the edges of the sheets (or trim to the basic measurement for the shape you wish to make). Gather up and reuse the trimmings if they are not too flour coated or have not dried out too much. For most shapes you will need to let the dough sheets rest and dry a little (about 5-10 minutes) before forming into the shapes. How long will depend on the temperature and humidity in the room. The sheets do not want to become so dry as to crack, but dry enough to be sure that the surfaces are not tacky all over yet still pliable enough to shape. You will get an instinctive feel for this as you become more familiar with the pasta making process.

Once at this stage turn to the instructions for the specific shape of pasta you want to make according to the recipe you are following.

If you have more pasta dough than you need for the recipe you can keep any unrolled pasta well wrapped in plastic wrap in the fridge for a few days, though it is always nicest eaten on the day it is made.

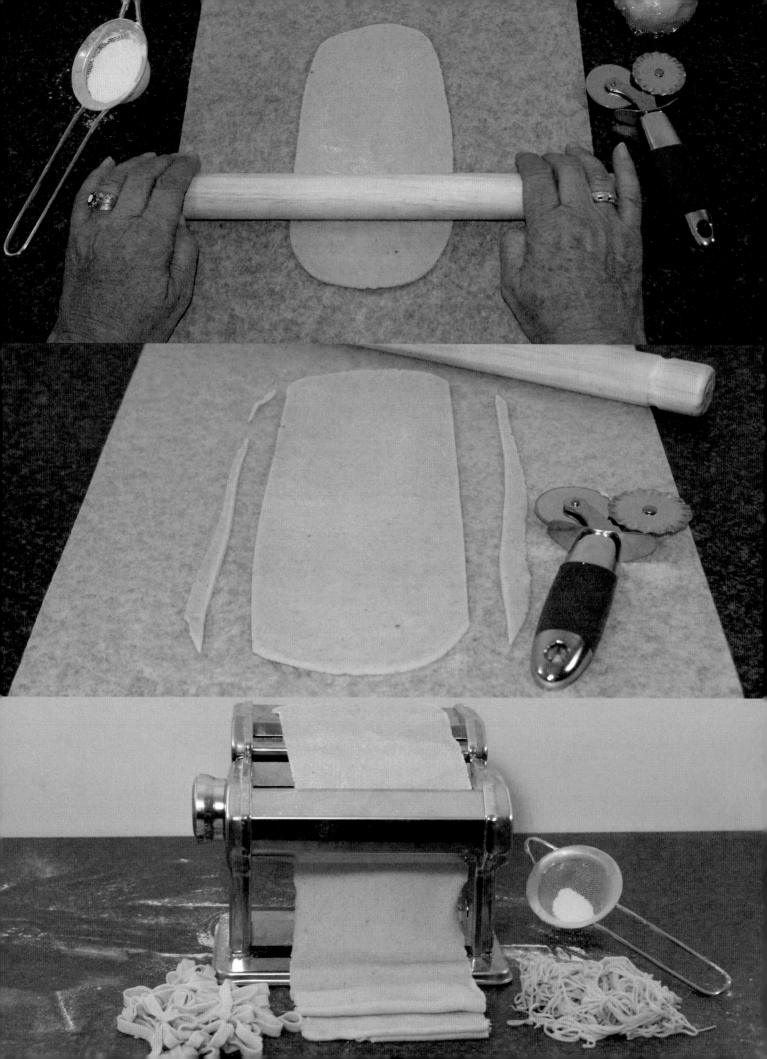

COLOURED AND FLAVOURED PASTA

Pasta need not always be beige because these days just about anything edible that can be pureed, comes in powder form, or as a coloured liquid can be added to pasta dough. The main benefit is to give the dough a different colour though some additions will also give a subtle flavour.
In the next few pages I will share my favourites including the most common colours as well as some suggestions for more daring flavours.

The following tips will help with making these delightful and often vibrant pastas:
If using a liquid or puree, the best way to evenly incorporate the colour or flavour is to beat it into the eggs before adding them to the dough, it can also help to gauge what strength of colour the resulting dough will be. The addition of flavourings may change the structure of the dough and make it more difficult to handle, roll out and often reduces the elasticity. Once you have some experience with plain pasta dough you will find it easier to judge how to get the texture of these doughs just right. You may have to add extra flour or water and you may not succeed in getting the sheet rolled quite as thin as you would one made from plain pasta dough. Anything you add should be powdered, pureed or chopped very finely. If any flavouring has lumps it will hinder your ability to roll out the dough thin enough to use, and make cutting it difficult.
Flavoured pastas are best used the day they are made. Most of the pastas made with vegetable purees are not recommended for drying. Turmeric, squid ink and chocolate pastas do however dry quite well if you want to keep them.

BEETROOT gives a fun colour that kids love to make shapes from. Even better, beetroot adds no discernable flavour to the finished dough. However, it is the least stable of the colours losing its brightness when the pasta is cooked resulting in a pale pink pasta. Best used with creamy sauces.

Proportions: 2 tablespoons for a full batch or 1 tablespoon for a half batch.

Preparation: It is best to use fresh cooked beetroot, peeled and then pureed. If using canned beetroot, choose baby beets and rinse well to remove any brine, drain then puree. Be careful using beetroot as it can stain clothes, benches and hands. Once incorporated into the dough it will no longer be a problem.

SPINACH obtains the most satisfactory dark green colour when made with powdered spinach. You can use well drained cooked fresh spinach, but the large amount you have to add to get a rich green colour affects the structure of the dough. This is a very versatile flavour and can be used with any sauce. I do not recommend you dry this pasta and it is best used on the day made.

Proportions for powder: 3-4 tablespoons for a full batch or 1½ tablespoons for a half batch.

Preparation: It is fairly easy to make your own spinach powder by hanging spinach up to dry in a hot dry place, using a dehydrator or in an oven set to very low for a few hours. Once totally dry break leaves off the stems and blend into a powder in a small spice grinder or kitchen whizz. Once powdered it keeps for a long time in an airtight container and then it is so easy to make spinach pasta whenever the inspiration strikes you.

CHOCOLATE despite what you might think does not make a sweet pasta. The use of pure baking cocoa gives a mild yet rich chocolate flavour and colour depending on the strength of the cocoa used. In Italy this pasta would be matched with a rich game meat sauce such as venison, wild boar or rabbit. Outside of Italy it might be more commonly found accompanied by sweet sauces. I suggest you try both as they are equally delicious.

Proportions: 4 tablespoons for a full batch or 1½ tablespoons for a half batch.

Preparation: Measure the flour for the dough then remove as many tablespoons of the flour as you will replace with cocoa. Cocoa absorbs more water than flour so substituting the flour for cocoa removes the need to add too much extra water to the dough. Sieve the cocoa powder into the flour to make sure there are no lumps. Mix thoroughly then make dough as normal.

HERBS fresh or dried, on their own or in combination add a lovely green fleck and punchy burst of flavour to the dough. Parsley, basil, oregano, marjoram, sage, thyme, rosemary, dill, tarragon and chives are all excellent in pasta dough. Pair the herbs with the flavour of the sauce you intend to serve.

Proportions: 2 tablespoons of dried herbs or 4 tablespoons of fresh herbs for a full batch, or 1 tablespoon of dried or 2 tablespoons of fresh herbs for a half batch.

Preparation: Finely chop the herbs, as if they are left too large it will be difficult to cut the dough especially if making spaghetti or fettuccine.

SQUID INK is one flavour ingredient that is worth the effort to source as the end result is a stunning jet black pasta that looks amazing with almost any sauce especially seafood. Most delicatessens or specialty food shops will stock squid ink. Quite a versatile pasta, it is beautiful with seafood, creamy sauces, in salads and is also excellent as ravioli with pumpkin filling.

Proportions: 8g packet or 2 teaspoons for a full batch, 4g packet or 1 teaspoon for a half batch.

Preparation: When preparing the dough a good quality ink will smell a little like the sea but this aroma is often not detectable in the cooked pasta. It all depends on the source of the ink what the end flavour will be. You may think the ink would stain your hands and bench but it does not, though I would be careful with the pure ink near your clothes.

CARROT is much like spinach pasta where dried, powdered carrot gives a much more defined colour, but you can use puree if you prefer.

Proportions: 4 tablespoons powder for a full batch or 2 tablespoons powder for a half batch.

Preparation: Mix powder with the flour, or puree with the eggs, then make dough as per usual instructions.

TOMATO is lovely in salads, or just with olive oil, salt and pepper. Pasta made with tomato is usually more orangey than red and can be quite subtle in flavour depending on the strength of the tomato paste. It can also be used with creamy sauces which allow the dough's colour to stand out.

Proportions: 2 tablespoons paste for a full batch or 1 tablespoon paste for a half batch.

Preparation: Use any brand of tomato paste or make a puree of sundried tomatoes for a more robust flavour. Mix with the oil when making the dough.

GROUND TURMERIC spice adds a lovely yellow colour to your pasta dough and it's a lot cheaper than using saffron. Turmeric is also well known for its myriad of health benefits. Fantastic with any sauce.
Proportions: 1 teaspoon for a full batch or ½ teaspoon for a half batch. Vary amount depending on the strength of colour you desire.
Preparation: Mix spice powder with the flour then make dough as per usual instructions.

RED CAPSICUM adds a burst of orangey red colour to pasta as well as a spicy sweet flavour. Used with any sauce, it is also especially good in a pasta salad.
Proportions: 2 tablespoons for a full batch or 1 tablespoon for a half batch.
Preparation: Use either raw or roasted capsicum blended into a fine puree. Drain puree to remove any excess water before using.

OTHER FLAVOURS you might like to try, remembering the general rules. If it is a puree, use 2 tablespoons for a full batch and 1 tablespoon for a half batch. For powders use 3-4 tablespoons for a full batch and 1½ tablespoons for a half batch, unless it's a very strong flavour like chilli or wasabi, then I suggest trying a ratio of teaspoons or less first until you decide how strong you like it.

Mushroom: Great for its earthy flavour it goes well with creamy or stock based sauces.
Red wine: Use the fruity aspects of the wine to subtly enhance rich meaty sauces.
Onion, leek or garlic: Great for a subtle flavour especially in Macaroni Cheese or Pasta Bake.
Lemon or lemon pepper: A bit of zingy fun, great in a pasta salad.
Black olive or tapenade: A rich, salty, black-flecked pasta fabulous with cheese sauces, tomatoes and in salads.
Green capsicum or peas can be a substitute for spinach.
Edible flower petals are another interesting colour option.
Fusion food: Try curry powder pasta and a coconut sauce or wasabi pasta with an asian inspired creation, chilli (fresh or dried) or cajun spiced pasta with chicken sauces, even blue corn pasta can be fun for children's parties if you can find blue corn.
Also for children's parties: Place several drops of food colouring in a resealable bag, add cooked pasta, seal, shake then serve. This method of colouring pasta can result in a rainbow of glorious colours, though I do prefer using natural colourings when possible.

STRIPED OR DUAL COLOURED PASTA

This style of pasta can look amazing when served with a minimalist sauce. The most effective types of pasta to make are fettuccine, pappardelle, farfalle and ravioli. The down side is that it's a bit fiddly to do and trimmings can not be rerolled.

To make pasta that is a different colour on each side:
Roll out two equal sized oblongs of different coloured dough to 4 card thickness using as little flour as possible. Trim to make them exactly the same size. Then immediately place one oblong on top of the other, gently press together with a rolling pin. Providing the dough has not dried out or been overly floured then they should stick together. Using either a rolling pin or a machine roll out to 3 card thickness, then cut into fettuccine or pappardelle as normal.

For stripy pasta there are two methods:
When the stripes are to show on both sides:
Roll out two equal sized oblongs of different coloured dough to 4 card thickness using as little flour as possible. Trim to make them exactly the same size. With a pasta wheel cut each oblong into strips and then make a new oblong by laying down alternating colours of pasta side by side, leaving no gaps. Gently roll with a rolling pin to make the cut edges join together and then continue rolling out to the desired thickness using either a rolling pin or a machine. Use for making farfalle.

When the stripes only need to show on one side:
Roll out two oblongs of different coloured dough to 4 card thickness using as little flour as possible, cut to the same length. The accent colour can be a narrower oblong. Cut the narrower oblong into even strips and then place the pasta strips on top of the other (still whole) oblong where you want the stripes to be. Gently roll with a rolling pin to make the strips fuse together and then continue rolling out to the desired thickness using either a rolling pin or a machine. Use for making ravioli.

Cook's Tip:
The stripy on one side pasta is the easier of the two stripy pastas to make.

LONG PASTAS

PICI originating in Siena, Tuscany, is a thick hand rolled pasta that is a lot of fun to make, and is so easy children can do it too. A substantial pasta it is best paired with rich hearty, meaty sauces or used in pasta bakes.

To make: Take a cherry tomato sized pinch of pasta dough, rolling it out between your hands to form a sausage shape (much like you may have done with play dough as a child). Place on a bench and continue to roll out using the flat of your hands until approximately ½cm (¼") thick (about half the thickness of a ball point pen) and about 30cm (12") long.

SPAGHETTI translates to mean "little or thin strings". Excellent when used with olive oil based lighter sauces like pesto. Outside of Italy it is often used in a very non-traditional way with bolognaise sauce or meatballs.

To make: Divide your dough into even egg size pieces and roll out to 3 card thickness. Spaghetti is best cut using a pasta machine attachment as it's very hard to cut fine enough by hand; you are more likely to get nearer to a linguine in width. If you are making spaghetti using a machine attachment and the dough doesn't cut properly then it's too damp, let it rest a little longer. If it cracks then it has become too dry. Spaghetti is best cooked as soon after cutting as possible.

LINGUINE, BAVETTE & TRENETTE are all names for 4mm wide, long, flat pasta. Linguine translates to "little tongues" in Italian. Linguine originated in Genoa, in the Liguria region of Italy. Like spaghetti this pasta is best served with lighter sauces.

TAGLIATELLE (tagliare – "to cut") sits in width between linguine and fettuccine, and is a width better suited to cutting by hand than are the thinner ones described above.

FETTUCCINE at 6-8mm wide is known as "little ribbons" and due to its extra width can cope with creamier sauces and ragùs. This is a fantastic and versatile pasta shape that is also easy to cut by hand.

To make linguine, tagliatelle or fettuccine: Divide your dough into egg size pieces and roll out to 3 card thickness. Commonly pasta machines come with a fettuccine and spaghetti cutting attachment, however if you want linguine or tagliatelle you can with a bit of practice cut the different widths by hand.

To cut by hand roll out to 3 card thickness, trim into an oblong shape, leave to dry for approximately 10 minutes. Dust with flour and fold the dough into a zigzag then cut to the required width with a knife or pasta wheel. With floured hands "toss" the cut strands to separate. Best if cooked soon after cutting or hang strands up to dry so the strands don't stick together.

QUADRETTI literally "little squares" are hand cut from the ends of fettuccine or tagliatelle. They are fantastic for keeping either dried (they dry quite quickly) or frozen ready as a quick addition to soups. A great way to use up any left over bits of dough, if you add a little quadretti to your collection each time you make pasta then there will always be some on hand for making soup.

To make: Cut the pasta into fettuccine or tagliatelle and then cut across the strands of pasta the opposite way to make little squares. Spread out on a tea towel to dry.

QUICK NO COOK SAUCES - PASTA CON SALSA CRUDA

A lot of Italian pasta sauces are very easy to prepare so when you just can't face cooking but still want something packed full of flavour for dinner I suggest you try one of the following no cook sauces.

Ensure all the ingredients are at room temperature before preparing and serve with your favourite pasta. Proportions will depend entirely on how strongly flavoured you like your sauce to be and how many you are serving. I recommend spaghetti and fettuccine as a quick to make pasta match for these sauces.

To cook the pasta: Place a large pot of heavily salted water on to boil using a high heat. When the pasta water is boiling rapidly, add the spaghetti or fettuccine, immediately stirring to separate the strands. Boil uncovered until the pasta is al dente (2-4 minutes). Drain, reserving some of the pasta water, then toss through your chosen sauce from the recipes below.

PESTO PASTA PRONTO

Mix basil pesto with a little of the pasta cooking water to thin and warm the pesto then toss through the pasta, serve topped with extra basil if you have it.

CHUNKY DIPS

With flavours like sun dried tomato, roasted capsicum or feta and spinach these dips make an excellent stir through sauce. As they often also have parmesan in them you won't even need extra cheese for serving though I do admit to often grating some on top anyway! Mix with a little of the pasta cooking water to thin and warm the dip and to help it toss through the pasta. To serve you can fancy it up by adding halved cherry tomatoes or a little torn prosciutto.

CACAO E PEPE

A minimalist pasta dish of Roman origin.

The simplest of dressings is a glug of the best olive oil you can afford seasoned with freshly ground black pepper and tossed through with generous helpings of grated pecorino cheese. Only drain the pasta quickly so some of the water still clings to it, this will help melt the cheese and make it stick to the pasta.

PASTA AI QUATTRO FORMAGGI

Sauce serves 4

Toss 4 tablespoons of butter through drained pasta and add ½ cup each of finely grated parmesan and cheddar cheese and then add your choice of crumbled blue cheese, feta, goat's cheese or tiny chunks of camembert. If needed mix with a little of the pasta water to get the right consistency. Season with salt and pepper and serve immediately.

TWO TOMATO SALSA

In a serving bowl put finely diced fresh and sun dried tomatoes then stir through a couple of tablespoons of hot pasta water. Toss the hot pasta in a little olive oil then add to the tomatoes, throw in some toasted pine nuts and fresh basil then crumble over feta or add pieces of mozzarella. Excellent served hot or cold.

SPAGHETTI CARBONARA

Such a popular Italian pasta dish, no pasta book would be complete without it. The recipe is originally said to hail from Rome and is often made there with fettuccine.

Serves 4

1 batch spaghetti (p.28)

8 slices streaky bacon
3 eggs
50g parmesan (grated)
Salt & pepper (to taste)
70-100ml cream (double cream is best)
Pinch grated nutmeg

Ingredient Note:
You can substitute finely grated extra tasty cheddar cheese for the parmesan, if you can't find affordable good quality parmesan.

1. Place a large pot of heavily salted water on to boil using a high heat.
2. Dice the bacon and fry till crispy in a frying pan large enough to toss the pasta in later, set pan aside when cooked.
3. In a bowl, beat together the eggs, cheese, cream, nutmeg, salt and pepper.
4. When the pasta water is boiling rapidly add the spaghetti, immediately stirring to separate the strands.
5. Boil uncovered for only 2 minutes as the pasta will keep cooking in the carbonara sauce.
6. Drain, reserving some of the pasta water.
7. Put the frying pan with the bacon cubes back on the heat and add the drained pasta, tossing well to coat with the bacon juices. Add a little of the reserved pasta water if necessary.
8. Take the pan off the heat again and add the egg and cheese mixture, quickly tossing everything to mix through thoroughly so that the eggs don't scramble.
9. Serve immediately.

WARM SPAGHETTI & ZUCCHINI SALAD

This is a lovely light dish which works beautifully with tomato or capsicum flavoured pasta.

Serves 4

½ batch spaghetti (p.28)

3 medium zucchini
1 large lemon (juice & zest)
4 T olive oil
1 cup parmesan (grated)
**2 large handfuls flat leaf parsley
   (optional)**
Salt & pepper (to taste)

Ingredient Note:
If your zucchini are young enough you can use the whole zucchini. If you use larger ones (or a marrow) leave out the very seedy bit in the middle.

1. Place a large pot of heavily salted water on to boil using a high heat.
2. Wash the zucchini then dry and slice with a julienne peeler to make "spaghetti" strips of zucchini.
3. In a bowl whisk the lemon juice, lemon zest, oil, finely diced parsley, salt and pepper.
4. Add the strips of zucchini to the bowl and stir to combine. Leave to marinate while you prepare and cook the spaghetti.
5. When the pasta water is boiling rapidly, add the spaghetti, immediately stirring to separate the strands. Boil uncovered until the pasta is al dente (2-3 minutes).
6. Remove the zucchini from the marinade and place into a large salad bowl. Combine with the drained spaghetti then pour over the marinade, add the parmesan, then toss until everything is coated.

Cook's Tip:
You can also create julienne like zucchini by lying a box grater on its side and grate by holding the long side of the zucchini against the grater, or use a peeler and make long peeled strips.

SPAGHETTI BOLOGNAISE

The bolognaise sauce in "Spag Bol" bears little resemblance to its namesake originating from Bologna, Italy. The original sauce (Ragù alla Bolognese) was not made with minced meat as we use today; instead, whole meat, usually beef or veal was chopped finely with a knife and cooked for several hours to tenderize it. However, even in Italy the sauce differs from region to region, so much so, that in 1982 an official recipe was deposited in the Chamber of Commerce of Bologna by the "Accademia Italiana della Cucina". In Italy it would never be served with spaghetti as that is considered too thin to hold the meat which will as a result all end up at the bottom of your plate. The dish we enjoy would be more accurately called "spaghetti with meat sauce", and every family will no doubt have their favourite version. The recipe below is loosely based on the official 1982 Ragù with my suggestions for some tasty additions. Feel free to include all or none of them.

Serves 4

1 batch spaghetti (p.28)

500g beef mince
100g pancetta finely diced (optional)
410g can tomato puree
1–2 cups soffritto
100ml red wine (optional)
3 bay leaves
3 cloves garlic (optional)
100ml milk (optional)
Salt & pepper (to taste)

Ingredient Note:
If you don't have soffritto use 1 onion and 1-2 medium carrots finely diced, cooking these with the mince.

Instead of pancetta use 2 t bacon stock or 8 rashers streaky bacon finely diced.

In place of tomato puree use 400g can tomatoes blended smooth and 2 T tomato paste.

Feel free to also add chopped herbs such as parsley or oregano if desired.

1. In a large frying pan cook the mince until nicely browned and add pancetta if using and fry for a few extra minutes.
2. Add in the tomato puree and all the remaining ingredients you are using and mix thoroughly.
3. Add enough water to cover the mince and let simmer on a low heat for a minimum of 20 minutes. The sauce can be simmered for up to 4 hours but keep checking the water level and top up as necessary.
4. Place a large pot of heavily salted water on to boil using a high heat.
5. When the pasta water is boiling rapidly, add the spaghetti, immediately stirring to separate the strands. Boil uncovered until the pasta is al dente (2-3 minutes).
6. Drain the pasta, reserving a little of the cooking water. Add some of the water to the sauce mixture and stir through.
7. Toss a little olive oil through the pasta then serve with the sauce piled high on top.
8. Though not traditional sprinkle with some grated extra tasty cheddar cheese, or parmesan if desired and enjoy.

Cook's Tip:
The milk adds a mellower flavour, taking the edge off the acidity of the tomatoes and also allegedly helping tenderize the meat (important in the days before mincers and meat was "minced" with a knife), but in my opinion it is just as enjoyable without the milk, making the dish dairy free.

FETTUCCINE ALFREDO

A decadent and delicious sauce that is worth the calories every now and again. But if you just can't bring yourself to make the full cream version a lighter alternative is given in the variations.

Serves 4

1 batch fettuccine (p.29)

4 T butter
¾ cup cream
1 cup parmesan (grated)
Salt & pepper (to taste)
Handful flat leaf parsley or
   chives (optional)

Cook's Tip:
Always keep the sauce cooking at a low heat, if it boils it will spoil.

1. Place a large pot of heavily salted water on to boil using a high heat.
2. When the pot is almost boiling begin to prepare the sauce.
3. In a saucepan on a low heat melt the butter then pour in the cream stirring to combine. As the sauce gently heats up it should thicken.
4. When the pasta water is boiling rapidly, add the fettuccine, immediately stirring to separate. Boil uncovered until the pasta is al dente (3-4 minutes).
5. When the pasta is almost cooked add the parmesan to the sauce and stir through to combine.
6. Drain the pasta and toss through the sauce, season with salt and pepper and freshly chopped herbs if desired.

Variations:
For a lighter sauce use ½ cup milk (full milk works best) and ½ cup plain Greek yoghurt to replace the cream and butter. If you like you could also reduce the amount of cheese to ½ cup.
1 t garlic salt adds an extra flavour kick to either sauce.

BASIC PICI PASTA BAKE

I don't know where this recipe came from but it has been in our family for many years going through various adaptations during that time. It is a great go-to recipe when everyone has had a busy day, the children are wanting attention and you haven't had time to go to the supermarket. It is quick and easy to throw together with a few store cupboard essentials and children will love helping make the pici. It's a great way to keep them occupied while you make the sauce.

Serves 4

½-1 batch pici (p.28)

500g beef mince
1 cup soffritto (or 1 large onion)
1 T brown sugar
1 t curry powder
1 t mustard powder
400g can chopped tomatoes
1 T tomato paste
Handful flat leaf parsley
½-1 cup cheese

Ingredient Note:
The quantity of pasta you choose to use depends on the appetites you are feeding. Though if you do have any leftovers it makes a fantastic lunch for the next day.

1. In a large frying pan, fry the mince and soffritto (or diced onion) until all nicely browned.
2. In a tiny bowl mix together the brown sugar, curry powder and mustard then sprinkle over the mince mixture, mixing well and fry for 3 more minutes stirring constantly.
3. Add the canned tomatoes then half fill the can with water. Add this along with the tomato paste and chopped parsley then stir through.
4. Lower the heat to a simmer, stirring occasionally.
5. Place a large pot of heavily salted water on to boil using a high heat.
6. When the pasta water is boiling rapidly, add the pici, immediately stirring to separate. Boil uncovered until the pasta is very al dente (5-7 minutes).
7. Drain pasta and mix through the mince, don't worry if the pasta breaks up a bit.
8. Put the mixture into a large baking dish and sprinkle a layer of cheese over the top.
9. Grill (broil) until golden brown and bubbly.
10. Serve accompanied with a green salad.

SPAGHETTI & MEATBALLS

This dish is American–Italian in origin and has been accepted by many as a classic pasta dish. However, you won't find it in Italian restaurants unless they are catering to tourists! Meatballs do exist in Italy but are usually much smaller than those typically used in this recipe and would be served as a dish on their own most commonly as a main course and never with the pasta. That aside it is a fantastic, budget friendly and filling family meal.

Serves 4

1 batch spaghetti (p.28)

1 cup soffritto
250g beef mince
250g pork mince
1-2 eggs
400g can chopped tomatoes
2 T tomato paste
2 t beef or bacon stock
2 cloves garlic (optional)
2 handfuls fresh herbs
  (finely chopped)
Salt & pepper (to taste)

Ingredient Note:
Fresh parsley, oregano, marjoram and basil used individually or together add a lovely flavour to this dish.

1. Set aside ½ cup of soffritto for the sauce.
2. In a large bowl put the remaining soffritto, both minces, and the eggs. Mix thoroughly using your hands, squeezing and squishing. The pork mince is helpful here as it is "stickier" than beef mince.
3. Shape into meatballs the size of a walnut and put in a clean shallow dish. Cover with cling wrap and put in the fridge to rest for at least 30 minutes.
4. In a large frying pan brown the meatballs then remove from the pan.
5. Add the soffritto to the frying pan (cooking for a few minutes if raw) then add the tomatoes and other ingredients, stirring well.
6. Add at least 1 tomato can of water to the pan and stir again, then place the meatballs back in the pan. The sauce should at least half cover the meatballs, if not add some more water.
7. Let them simmer for 20-30 minutes, turning occasionally and adding further water as needed to keep the meatballs half covered.
8. While the sauce simmers, place a large pot of heavily salted water on to boil using a high heat.
9. If you are not sure if the meatballs are cooked through, take one out and cut it in half to check. If the sauce seems a little too runny, turn up the heat and let the sauce boil until it has reached the right consistency.
10. When the pasta water is boiling rapidly (and the meatballs are cooked through), add the spaghetti to the pasta pot, immediately stirring to separate the strands. Boil uncovered until the pasta is al dente (2-3 minutes).
11. Drain the pasta reserving a little of the cooking water to add to the sauce mixture if it has became too thick.
12. Toss the pasta in a little olive oil to coat it then serve the sauce ladled on top of the pasta and the meatballs stacked high. Sprinkle over some additional fresh herbs if you like.

SUMMER SPAGHETTI WITH NZ GREEN LIPPED MUSSELS

One of my favourite ways to eat mussels is in this fresh summer sauce. The spaghetti soaks up all the wonderful juices and it's a great dish for a casual get together with friends.

Serves 4

1 batch spaghetti (p.28)

1kg NZ green lipped mussels
**   (5-6 per person)**
½ red capsicum
5 spring onions
2 large handfuls parsley
1 large lemon (juice & zest)
1 T olive oil
1 cup white wine
2-3 cloves garlic (crushed)
1 t red chilli flakes (optional)
Salt & pepper (to taste)
1 cup cherry tomatoes

Ingredient Note:
NZ green lipped mussels are one of the largest in the world so
1kg would be about 20 mussels.
If you can't get NZ green lipped mussels, substitute for 1kg of your local mussels. You will need to adjust the cooking time if using smaller mussels.

1. Clean the mussels by scrubbing the shells under running water and pulling the beard towards the hinge to remove it. This step is important as the mussels will be cooked in the pasta sauce. Discard any mussels that have cracked or broken shells, and any open mussels that don't close up when you tap them as these are not safe to eat.
2. Dice the capsicum, spring onions and parsley. Set aside three tablespoons with some lemon zest for a garnish.
3. In a very large frying pan, one that has a lid, heat the olive oil and lightly fry the garlic, lemon, capsicum, spring onions, parsley and chilli flakes.
4. Add the lemon juice, white wine, salt and pepper and simmer gently until the liquid has reduced by half.
5. During this time place a large pot of heavily salted water on to boil using a high heat. It should be boiling before you start cooking the mussels.
6. Add the mussels to the frying pan and put on the lid. Set a timer for 5 minutes. At this mark add the spaghetti to the boiling water pot, immediately stirring to separate the strands. Boil uncovered until the pasta is very al dente (2 minutes).
7. Somewhere between 5 and 7 minutes the mussels should have fully opened indicating that they are cooked. Once that happens, remove them from the frying pan, discarding any that did not open as those are unsafe to eat. Also discard the empty half of the opened mussel shells.
8. Drain the pasta, reserving some of the cooking water.
9. Add the drained pasta to the frying pan and toss to coat with the sauce, adding a little pasta water to thin the sauce if needed. The pasta will cook a little from the heat of the sauce.
10. Add the half shell mussels back in, sprinkle with the halved cherry tomatoes and the reserved garnish. Serve.

Cook's Tip:
The timing is critical in this dish to ensure the mussels and pasta are both served at their optimum.

FETTUCCINE WITH BRUSSELS SPROUTS

If you are not a fan of brussels sprouts this recipe might just convert you. Here they are perfectly balanced with crunchy nuts, crispy salty bacon and a pungent lemony sauce. I know a few fussy eaters who said they would never eat brussels sprouts that came back begging for seconds.

Serves 4

1 batch fettuccine (p.29)

12 brussels sprouts
6 strips streaky bacon
½-1 cup walnuts (chopped)
Salt & pepper (to taste)
1 lemon (juiced)
1 T olive oil
Parmesan (optional)

Ingredient Note:
You can substitute the walnuts for cashews or pine nuts if you prefer.

1. Place a large pot of heavily salted water on to boil using a high heat.
2. Chop the walnuts into rough pieces and set aside.
3. Peel off the outer leaves of the brussels sprouts and discard, then cut the brussels in half and shred finely.
4. In a frying pan on medium heat fry the bacon rashers. Once cooked remove and set aside.
5. Add the brussels to the pan to fry. While the brussels fry chop the bacon into bite size bits.
6. When the pasta water is boiling rapidly add the fettuccine, immediately stirring to separate the strands. Boil uncovered until the pasta is al dente (3-4 minutes).
7. Mix the lemon juice, olive oil, salt and pepper together in a large bowl.
8. Drain the pasta and immediately add to the bowl, tossing gently to coat the strands in the lemony dressing. Add in the cooked bacon bits and brussels sprouts and mix through.
9. Serve with shaved parmesan.

FRITTATA DI SPAGHETTI

A fantastic way to use up leftovers, this frittata is delicious served hot for a filling lunch or to pack in a picnic basket once cold. If you have any to spare it's also perfect to pop in a lunchbox.

Serves 6

2-3 cups cooked spaghetti

6 eggs
6 T milk (or water or cream)
Salt & pepper (to taste)
1 cup cheese (grated)
½ cup ham chunks
½ cup peas
6 sundried tomatoes (diced)
1 onion (diced)
Chives

Cook's Tip:
If you find the egg mixture has not covered all the ingredients whisk an additional egg with 1 T liquid and add to the dish before covering with cheese.

1. Turn on the oven to preheat to 200°C.
2. In a frying pan on medium heat cook the onion and ham and peas till all are warmed through and the onion is translucent.
3. In a large bowl beat the eggs with the milk, salt and pepper. Add in half of the cheese.
4. Add to the bowl the cooked spaghetti and the contents of the frying pan. Mix gently until well combined.
5. Choose an oven proof dish (a flan dish is ideal), oil well and then pour in the eggy mixture.
6. Ensure the mixture is spread evenly in the dish then sprinkle the remaining cheese over the top.
7. Fan bake at 200°C for 30 minutes until golden brown on top.
8. Let rest for 5 minutes before slicing if eating hot; otherwise wait until completely cold and then slice.

Variation:
Any of these combinations are also delicious in frittata. Just cook (if raw) and cut into bite size pieces before adding 1-2 cups in total:
Pumpkin & feta • Broccoli, chicken & blue cheese • Tuna & corn
Potato & canned salmon • Salami & peas • Bacon, leek & potato
Peas, carrots & bacon/ham • Parsnip, mushrooms & spinach
Asparagus & goats cheese • Roast vegetables

EGGS SPENEDICT

Eggs Benedict to me is synonymous with a great brunch but gluten free English muffins can be hard to come by. So one day, craving this dish, I thought, why not serve it on a bed of fresh spaghetti instead? All the flavours you would expect are still there - the creamy lemony hollandaise, smoked salmon, all topped with a perfectly poached egg. The spaghetti soaks up the hollandaise and mops up any egg yolk just like a muffin would. What more could you ask for? The addition of lightly sautéed new season asparagus gives the dish a spring colour and crunch. Try it you may fall in love!

Serves 6 for brunch

1 batch spaghetti (p.28)

1 bunch asparagus
1 T olive oil
Salt & pepper (to taste)
1 T white vinegar
6 fresh eggs
100g smoked salmon

For the hollandaise sauce:
150g butter
3 egg yolks (room temp)
1 large lemon (juice)
½ t salt

Ingredient Note:
If you prefer, use a ready prepared hollandaise sauce, warm before use.

Variations:
You can substitute spinach for the asparagus.
Leave out the salmon for a vegetarian option.
Also you can replace the smoked salmon with cooked fresh salmon or cooked streaky bacon if desired.

1. Place a large pot of heavily salted water on to boil using a high heat.
2. For the hollandaise sauce choose a small saucepan that you can rest a bowl on without it touching water in the bottom of the pot. Put a few centimetres of water in the saucepan, bring to the boil then put the bowl over the pan and turn down the heat.
3. Melt the butter in a separate pot, set aside.
4. Into the warm bowl (which is still on top of the pot) put the egg yolks, half the lemon juice and the salt. Whisk thoroughly until frothy.
5. Slowly add the melted butter to the bowl, whisking fast to stop the mixture separating. Continue until all the butter is added.
6. Thin the sauce with the remaining lemon juice until it reaches pouring consistency. Leave the sauce bowl on the pot and put to one side (off the heat) to stay warm.
7. To poach the eggs put a pot of water on to boil to which has been added the white vinegar.
8. Trim and discard the very ends from a bunch of thin new season asparagus. Then starting from the bottom, cut the asparagus into 2cm lengths until about 10cm from the tips. Sauté all the asparagus in a frying pan on medium heat with the olive oil, salt and pepper until lightly cooked but still crunchy.
9. Once the pasta water pot and the egg water pot are both boiling rapidly quickly break the eggs into the egg water and set a timer for 4 minutes. Add the pasta to the pasta pot, immediately stirring to separate the strands. Boil uncovered until al dente (2-3 minutes).
10. Drain and place pasta into a large pre-warmed bowl.
11. Remove the egg pot from the heat when the timer goes off and set to one side.
12. Drizzle the warm hollandaise sauce over the hot pasta reserving ¼ cup in a small serving jug. Add in the short bits of asparagus and if desired some little bits of salmon, mixing gently to distribute through the spaghetti.
13. Plate up the spaghetti in individual servings, on pre-warmed plates, laying the spears of asparagus on top of the spaghetti, then adding the salmon, and topping with a poached egg.
14. Serve with the reserved hollandaise sauce on the side.

QUADRETTI IN BROTH

This is a perfect soup for those recovering from the flu or a stomach ailment. Quick and easy to prepare as all ingredients can be made ahead of time and kept on hand for when you need this comforting broth.

Serves 4

½ cup quadretti (p.29)

4 cups chicken stock
1 cup soffritto (optional)

1. In a saucepan bring the stock to a boil, add soffritto.
2. Add the quadretti and cook until the pasta is soft.
3. Serve with fresh bread if desired.

Ingredient Note:
If you want a smoother broth blend the soffritto into the stock with a hand held blender.

TOMATO NOODLE SOUP

Need soup now? This noodle soup is perfect for a quick lunch on a cold winter's day, or as a snack to warm children up when they come home from school during winter.

Serves 4 for lunch

1 cup short noodles (p.28)

420g can condensed tomato
    soup
1 cup soffritto
2 handfuls fresh basil

Ingredient Note:
Make short noodles by cutting spaghetti into 2cm lengths. These can be made ahead of time and dried or frozen until needed.

1. In a saucepan heat the soup, one soup can full of water and the soffritto.
2. Once boiling rapidly add the noodles and cook for 2-3 minutes.
3. Stir in the torn fresh basil and serve.

Variations:
You can use 400g can chopped tomatoes blended smooth or a packet of tomato soup.

For Chicken Noodle Soup: Use 420g condensed chicken soup or a packet of chicken soup.

For Mushroom Soup: Use 420g can condensed mushroom soup or a packet of mushroom soup.

Cook's Tip:
Check to make sure the soup you use is gluten free.

PASTA AL NERO DI SEPPIA WITH PRAWNS

Squid ink pasta is my favourite of the coloured pastas as it's so simple to make yet stunning in presentation. There is virtually no detectable flavour of the squid left once you have cooked the pasta but as it is used here with prawns it would not matter if there was.

Serves 4

**1 batch squid ink spaghetti
   (p.22, 28)**

400g prawn cutlets
4 T butter
2-3 cloves garlic (crushed)
½ t dried chilli flakes (optional)
1 lemon (juice & zest)
½ red capsicum (cut into sticks)
1-2 zucchini (cut into sticks)
1 cup white wine

Cook's Tip:
The pasta will absorb the sauce so don't worry if it is quite runny.

1. Defrost the prawns if frozen.
2. Place a large pot of heavily salted water on to boil using a high heat.
3. When the pasta water is boiling rapidly, begin cooking the sauce.
4. In a large frying pan melt the butter then add garlic, chilli (if using), lemon juice and prawns.
5. Fry prawns for 1 minute turning often to coat in sauce then add the capsicum and zucchini and cook for 3-5 minutes until the prawns are cooked through (white/orange all over).
6. Add the spaghetti to the pasta pot when the prawns have 3 minutes left to cook. Immediately stirring to separate the strands. Boil uncovered until the pasta is quite al dente (2 minutes).
7. With 1 minute left to go add the white wine to the frying pan and mix well.
8. Drain the pasta, add to the frying pan and toss to coat with the sauce.
9. Serve immediately with lemon zest sprinkled on top.

Variation:
To make a beautiful entrée for 4-6 people, use 1-2 prawns per person and half the ingredients above. Use the capsicum and zucchini raw (instead of adding to the sauce) along with some fresh mixed green salad leaves to decorate the plate. Remove the prawns from the sauce when cooked. Plate the spaghetti and place prawns on top, sprinkle with lemon zest. If you don't like prawns, fresh salmon is a lovely substitute. If using you may have to allow extra cooking time.

CHOC ORANGE DELIGHT

This recipe allows each ingredient to shine yet combines them all to make a truly sensational dessert. I'm sure this will become a firm favourite in your house as it has in ours.

Serves 6 for dessert

½ batch chocolate fettuccine (p.21, 29)

1 orange (juice & zest)
½ cup orange marmalade
1 T Grand Marnier, Rum or Cointreau (optional)
2 T (25g) butter

Icecream or cream to serve (optional)

1. Place a large pot of heavily salted water on to boil using a high heat.
2. Zest the orange and set zest aside, then juice the orange.
3. Put the orange juice into a saucepan, add the marmalade and mix together over a medium heat until the marmalade has turned liquid.
4. Keep simmering until the sauce thickens then add the liqueur, stirring to combine.
5. Stir in the butter. As it melts the sauce will become nice and glossy.
6. Reduce to a low heat to keep warm while cooking the pasta.
7. When the pasta water is boiling rapidly, add the fettuccine, immediately stirring to separate. Boil uncovered until the pasta is al dente (3-4 minutes).
8. Drain the pasta well and then plate up. Spoon the orange sauce evenly over the pasta then top each plate with orange zest and if desired a small scoop of icecream or a drizzle of cream.

Variation:
It's also delicious served with chocolate flavoured cream. Warm ½ cup cream with 2 T chocolate spread until combined. Or for a healthier option serve with mint and Greek yoghurt.

FLAT PASTAS

LASAGNE has its origins in the Emilia-Romagna region of Italy and is now synonymous with the dish made using this pasta. Lasagnette is a narrower version of lasagne. Used with numerous different combinations of sauces to make a layered baked pasta dish.

To make: Determine the dish size that you will be using to bake the lasagne, then after rolling out the pasta to 3 card thickness cut to lengths that will fit the dish using either a fluted or straight edged pasta wheel.

SAGNARELLI are a great pasta to make if you want something quick but a little different. It is a flat pasta about 5cm (2″) long and 2-3cm (1″) wide with a fluted border.

To make: Roll out to 3 card thickness then cut pasta sheets to size using a fluted pastry wheel on all edges. Serve with a robust sauce.

MAFALDINE are strangely named "little queens" in honour of Princess Malfalda of Savoy. They are long ribbons of pasta with fluted or ruffled edges, like a very narrow lasagne. They can often also be referred to as reginette. Serve with robust sauces which have meat or vegetables in them.

To make mafaldine: Divide the dough into egg size sections and then roll out to 3 card thickness. Use a fluted pasta wheel to make the lengthwise cuts. This pasta absorbs a lot of water when cooking and expands a surprising amount widthwise. Keep this in mind when choosing how wide to cut the strands.

PAPPARDELLE are similar to mafaldine but without the fluted edge. This thick flat ribbon cut between 1cm and 3cm (1″) wide is named after the verb "pappare" to gobble up. Perfect to pair with robust sauces which have meat or vegetables in them.

To make pappardelle: Divide the dough into egg size sections and then roll out to 3 card thickness. Use a straight edged pasta wheel or knife to cut to desired width. Pappardelle will expand a surprising amount widthwise as it cooks so consider this when choosing how wide to cut the strands.

MALTAGLIATI meaning "poorly cut" is a perfect description for this pasta made with the roughly shaped scraps cut from the leftovers of your flat pasta sheets. Nice served with any sort of robust sauce or if cut quite small, use in a thick soup.

To make: Take flat sheet pasta scraps and cut into pieces at random angles with a straight edged pasta wheel.

LASAGNE

Lasagne is loved the world over. Although it takes time to prepare it can be made ahead of time, refrigerated, then put in the oven to bake later in the day. There has long been a debate about whether you need to precook the lasagne sheets. For dried pasta I always precooked them but since making fresh pasta I have just used as is. However you do need a little more liquid in your sauces if using the sheets uncooked. If pressed for time parboiling will help cut down the cooking time. If using fresh pasta you only need very short parboiling time (1 minute) then plunge into cold water to stop the cooking.

Serves 6

1 batch lasagne sheets (p.54)

1 batch bolognaise sauce (p.35)

Béchamel sauce:
4 T (50g) butter
4 T Pasta Blend (p.6)
4 cups milk
Salt & pepper (to taste)
1 cup cheddar cheese
   (grated)

Topping:
¼ cup extra tasty cheddar
   cheese (grated)

1. In a saucepan melt the butter over a low heat.
2. Add the Pasta Blend, and stir into the butter.
3. Remove from the heat and add the milk, bit by bit, stirring on each addition.
4. Return to the low heat and stir until thickened, adding salt and pepper.
5. Add the first measure of grated cheese and stir into the sauce until smooth. Set aside.
6. Turn the oven on to preheat to 180°C.
7. To assemble the lasagne, grease a deep lasagne dish then cut the pasta sheets to fit.
8. Put a layer of pasta sheets on the bottom of the dish.
9. Add a layer of béchamel sauce.
10. Then a layer of bolognaise sauce (see Ingredient Note p.57).
11. Top with another layer of lasagne sheets.
12. Continue until the dish is full, finishing with a layer of lasagne sheets topped with béchamel sauce and sprinkled with extra cheese.
13. Fan bake at 180°C for 45 minutes to 1 hour depending on the depth of your dish.
14. Take out of the oven and let sit for at least 10 minutes before cutting. Serve with a green salad.

GOURMET LASAGNE

I have made lasagne this way for as long as I can remember. It seems to take forever but the resulting dish is definitely worth it! I always tend to make twice as much, so I can put some in the freezer for when there's just no time to make it from scratch.

Serves 6-8

1 batch lasagne sheets (p.54)

1 batch bolognaise sauce (p.35)
6 cups béchamel sauce (p.56)
6-10 large spinach leaves
4 cups pumpkin (mashed)
¼ cup extra tasty cheddar cheese (grated)

Ingredient Note:
For a quick way to make mashed pumpkin see p.102.
If using bolognaise sauce prepared earlier, warm it up before using as it makes it easier to spread.

1. Cut any thick stalks out of the spinach and discard, set the leaves aside.
2. Turn oven on to preheat to 180°C.
3. To assemble the lasagne you will need a very deep dish. Grease the dish then cut the pasta sheets to fit.
4. Put a layer of pasta sheets on the bottom of the dish.
5. Add a layer of béchamel sauce.
6. Then a layer of bolognaise sauce.
7. Top with another layer of lasagne sheets.
8. Spread with a layer of mashed pumpkin and top with béchamel sauce.
9. Cover with another layer of lasagne sheets, then cover with spinach and a layer of béchamel sauce.
10. Add lasagne sheets then another layer of bolognaise sauce, topped with béchamel sauce.
11. Then a final layer of lasagne sheets, cover with the remaining béchamel sauce and sprinkle with the extra cheese.
12. Fan bake at 180°C for 45 minutes to 1 hour depending on the depth of your dish.
13. Take out of the oven and let sit for at least 10 minutes before cutting.

LASAGNE CUPS

Quick and impressive, these mini lasagne make a little go a long way. If I have some leftover pasta dough and bolognaise sauce, I will often make a few of these to pop in the freezer. Great for packed lunches or feeding unexpected guests.

To make 6

A large egg size piece of pasta dough

12 T bolognaise sauce (p.35)
6 T grated cheese
3 cherry tomatoes

6 ramekins
Baking paper

1. Turn the oven on to preheat to 180°C.
2. Cut a square of baking paper and fit inside the ramekins to determine what size the pasta squares will need to be. The paper needs to be big enough that the corners of the dough will stick up above the edge of the ramekin.
3. Roll the dough to 2 card thickness and then cut into squares the same size as the paper template. Repeat until there are 12 squares.
4. Grease the ramekin dishes with oil.
5. Place 2 squares of pasta into each ramekin and gently mould to the shape of the ramekin, turning the second square so that the corners stick up in a different spot.
6. Fill each ramekin with 2 tablespoons of bolognaise sauce. This should three quarters fill the ramekin, then sprinkle 1 tablespoon of cheese on top of each. Then top that with half a cherry tomato.
7. Cook at 180°C fan bake for 25-30 minutes. The cheese should be bubbly and golden all over and the pasta edges browned.
8. Serve in the ramekins. If you have any Lasagne Cups to spare they can be frozen once cold.

Variation:
Put 1 tablespoon of bolognaise sauce into the ramekin then add a layer of mashed pumpkin and/or cooked spinach and top with the remaining tablespoon of bolognaise sauce.

PASTA CON LE FAVE

Broad beans or fava beans are an acquired taste, one that I admit I did not have until quite recently. It was a Syrian grandmother's lovingly prepared dish of rice with double skinned fava beans that converted me. Once I realised the secret for enjoying broad beans was to eat them very young and tender or to skin the more mature, I began to really appreciate their nutty flavour. In this dish they truly excel.

Serves 4

1 batch maltagliati (p.54)

1½ cups young fresh broad beans (shelled)
2 cloves garlic (crushed)
1-2 large lemons (to taste)
8 rashers streaky bacon
4 T olive oil
½ cup parmesan (shaved)
Handful fresh mint or flat leaf parsley
Salt & pepper (to taste)

Ingredient Note:
It's important to use really young broad beans (fava beans) in this dish. If you cannot find young beans then you will need to double shell the beans by removing the outer bean pod and also the tougher grey bean skin after they have been boiled, to use only the tender inner beans.

1.   Place a large pot of heavily salted water on to boil using a high heat.
2.   Wash the lemons, dry and then using a sharp paring knife remove only the rind in long strips. Take care to avoid the pith. Once you have all the rind removed, julienne the rind as finely as possible.
3.   Dice the bacon rashers then lightly fry along with the lemon rind and half the olive oil in a frying pan over a low heat. Slow cooking will caramelize the lemon rind and bring a sweeter lemony flavour to the dish.
4.   In a saucepan simmer the broad beans for 2 minutes. Drain (skin if needed) and then add to the frying pan along with the crushed garlic, cooking for 2-3 minutes only.
5.   When the pasta water is boiling rapidly, add the maltagliati, immediately stirring to separate. Boil uncovered until the pasta is al dente (3-4 minutes).
6.   Drain the pasta and toss in the remaining olive oil.
7.   Deglaze the frying pan with the lemon juice then pour the sauce over the pasta, add the diced herb of your choice and toss to coat.
8.   Serve with the shaved parmesan, salt and pepper.

Variations:
Substitute peas or green beans for the broad beans.
Using 2 tablespoons of basil or parsley pesto to coat the pasta instead of olive oil and herbs is a delicious addition to the dish.

PAPPARDELLE WITH VENISON RAGÙ

This rich gamey casserole is a perfect match for chocolate pasta. Like a well-aged wine the combination of complex flavours will please any discerning palate.

Serves 4-6

1 batch chocolate pappardelle (p.21, 54)

1 cup red wine
¼ cup fresh rosemary
2 cloves garlic
400g venison (any stewing cut is fine)
10 button mushrooms or 5 field mushrooms (diced)
4 T cranberry jam
½ cup soffritto
Salt & pepper (to taste)
½ head broccoli

1. In a casserole dish mix the red wine, rosemary and garlic, then add the venison, stirring well until all the meat is coated in the wine. Cover and leave to marinate for at least 2 hours, mixing occasionally to ensure all the pieces of meat spend time in the marinade.

2. After the 2 hours marinating time is up, add in the remaining ingredients (except broccoli) and mix well.

3. Cover and put in the oven to fan bake at 160°C for 2½ hours minimum. Check the casserole, stirring from time to time. If the liquid looks to have evaporated too much, add in a little beef stock or water.

4. To test if the casserole is ready the meat should be so tender that it separates when you pull at it with two forks. Cooking time will vary depending on the cut of meat used.

5. Remove the meat from the casserole and using two forks shred all the meat into bite size pieces. Then return to the casserole and leave covered in the turned off oven while you prepare the pasta and broccoli.

6. Place a large pot of heavily salted water on to boil using a high heat.

7. Cut the broccoli into small florets and cook in another pot of boiling water until tender.

8. When the pasta water is boiling rapidly, add the pappardelle, immediately stirring to separate. Boil uncovered until the pasta is al dente (2-3 minutes).

9. Drain the pasta and place in a serving bowl, reserving a little of the cooking liquid.

10. Remove the casserole from the oven. Tip the liquid from the casserole over the pasta, toss to coat using the pasta water to thin the sauce if necessary. Spoon over the remaining meaty part of the casserole.

11. Serve with the broccoli and a little rosemary sprinkled on top.

Cook's Tip:
It is up to you if you marinate the venison in one large piece or dice it first, as later in the recipe you will remove the meat from the casserole and "pull" it by separating the fibres with two forks.

PAPPARDELLE WITH LEMON, OLIVES & THYME

Fabulously easy, this pasta dish is perfect to impress guests. For an extra wow factor, flavour the pasta dough with finely diced thyme. The sauce requires no cooking so you can have this served in the time it takes to cook the pasta.

Serves 4

1 batch pappardelle (p.54)

1 large handful fresh thyme sprigs
1 large lemon (juice & zest)
2 T olive oil (or the oil from the marinated olives)
Salt & pepper (to taste)
24 large pitted, marinated green olives

1. Place a large pot of heavily salted water on to boil using a high heat.
2. Remove the thyme leaves from the stems and place in a bowl.
3. Add the lemon juice, lemon zest, oil, salt and pepper and whisk together.
4. Dice half the olives and add to the sauce.
5. When the pasta water is boiling rapidly, add the pappardelle, immediately stirring to separate. Boil uncovered until the pasta is al dente (2-3 minutes).
6. Drain pasta then put in the serving bowl, pour over sauce and gently toss the pasta. Sprinkle over the whole olives and serve immediately with grated parmesan if desired.

Variation:
400g of shredded cooked chicken adds flavour and protein to this dish. If desired warm the chicken before adding to the pasta.

TUBULAR PASTAS

Tubular pastas require a little more time to shape but are well worth the effort for the variety of dishes they enable you to make.

CANNELLONI are typically filled with spinach and ricotta or meat and cheese and cooked in a tomato and/or béchamel sauce. Translated they are "large reeds" which seems very appropriate.

To make: Roll out the dough to 3 card thickness. There are two ways to fill the cannelloni. Place the filling along the length of a strip of pasta that is 15cm (6") wide and then carefully roll around the filling, then cut into even sections to make cannelloni. Or cut the pasta strip into rectangles 10cm x 15cm (4" x 6"), or to fit the width of your baking dish. Then put a fat sausage size amount of filling in from the edge and across the shorter width of each one. Roll the pasta around to encase the "sausage", it should overlap by a few centimetres. Put in the dish seam side down.

DITALI are a multipurpose mini tube shape meaning "thimbles" in Italian. Ditalini are smaller, but it is the larger ditaloni that are easiest to make at home. Perfect in homemade "macaroni" cheese, soups and salads. Making actual macaroni elbows at home is only possible with an extruding device attached to a kitchen mixer.

To make ditaloni: Roll out the pasta sheets to 4 card thickness then using a ruler and a flat pasta wheel cut into approximately 2cm x 3cm (1") pieces. Next roll each rectangle round a 6mm (¼") pasta shaping pin (or a knitting needle) to form tubes 2cm (1") wide. Allow to dry for at least 30 minutes (or overnight) on a clean tea towel before cooking.

GARGANELLI are the homemade equivalent to penne, though in commercially dried pasta both shapes exist, at home penne requires an extruder whereas garganelli can be made by hand. Garganelli come in both a ridged and smooth version and can be made smaller if you wish. When shaping they turn out a bit larger in diameter than the shaping pin. The ridges are particularly suited for trapping sauces, so this is the shape to use with thick, chunky sauces and in pasta bakes.

To make garganelli: Roll out to 3 card thickness then cut squares of 5cm x 5cm (2" x 2"). A smooth version is made by letting the cut pasta dry a little then roll diagonally across the square using a 6mm (¼") pasta shaping pin (or knitting needle). The ridged version uses a garganelli board, which is a small board with grooves for shaping the pasta, also used when making gnocchi. Position the board with the ridges aligned away from you. Place the pasta diagonally on the board and with a gentle downwards pressure roll the pin across the pasta away from you to create the ridges, then pull up the far corner and wrap around the pin and roll towards you. When almost complete press lightly to stick the corner of the pasta. Gently slide off the pin and allow to dry for at least 30 minutes (or overnight) on a clean tea towel.

CANNELLONI WITH 3 FILLINGS

A dish that is most commonly eaten at festive occasions, cannelloni is a fantastic choice for feeding a crowd. Like lasagne it can be made ahead, refrigerated and cooked later the same day. Cannelloni can be filled with numerous different combinations so feel free to experiment. Here are three of my favourite recipes to get you started.

BEEF CANNELLONI

Serves 4-5

½ batch cannelloni (p.66)

410g can tomato puree (passata)
Big handful fresh basil or flat leaf parsley
1 batch bolognaise sauce (p.35)
2 cups béchamel sauce (p.56)
1 cup cheese

1. Turn oven on to preheat to 180°C.
2. Cover the base of the dish with half the tomato puree, sprinkle over chopped green herbs.
3. Fill the cannelloni with fat sausage size amounts of the filling.
4. Roll up and place the filled cannelloni in the dish seam side down.
5. Cover with the remaining tomato puree, spoon over the béchamel sauce then top with grated cheese.
6. Fan bake at 180°C for 30-40 minutes until pasta is tender and the topping is bubbling and golden.
7. Remove from oven and let rest for 10 minutes before serving.

SPINACH CANNELLONI

Serves 4-5

½ batch cannelloni (p.66)

350g frozen spinach
500g cream cheese
Grated nutmeg (to taste)
410g can tomato puree (passata)
Big handful fresh basil or flat leaf parsley
2 cups béchamel sauce (p.56)
1 cup cheese

Ingredient Note:
You can use fresh spinach in place of the frozen spinach, remove the stems and wilt before using.

1. Turn oven on to preheat to 180°C.
2. Defrost the frozen spinach, strain to remove excess water then chop finely.
3. Put spinach in a bowl with the cream cheese and nutmeg and mix together until well combined.
4. Cover the base of the dish with half the tomato puree, sprinkle over chopped herbs.
5. Then fill the cannelloni with fat sausage size amounts of the filling.
6. Roll up and place the filled cannelloni in the dish seam side down.
7. Cover with the remaining tomato puree, spoon over the béchamel sauce then top with grated cheese.
8. Fan bake at 180°C for 30-40 minutes until pasta is tender and the topping is bubbling and golden.
9. Remove from oven and let rest for 10 minutes before serving.

Variation:
Finely dice a cooked chicken breast and add to the filling.

SALMON CANNELLONI

Serves 4-5

½ batch cannelloni (p.66)

1 leek (optional)
415g can salmon
250g cream cheese
1 large lemon (juice & zest)
Pepper (to taste)
Big handful flat leaf parsley, dill
    or chives
4 cups béchamel sauce (p.56)
    (omit the cheese)

Ingredient Note:
This looks sensational when made
with black squid ink pasta.

1. Turn oven on to preheat to 180°C.
2. Finely chop the leek and put into a large bowl.
3. Drain the salmon then add to the leek along with the cream cheese, lemon zest and 1 T lemon juice. Mix thoroughly until all well combined.
4. Make béchamel sauce adding in the remaining lemon juice and pepper then stir through the chopped herbs. Cover the base of the dish with half of the sauce.
5. Fill the cannelloni with fat sausage size amounts of the filling.
6. Roll up and place the filled cannelloni in the dish seam side down.
7. Cover with the remaining béchamel sauce.
8. Fan bake at 180°C for 30-40 minutes until pasta is tender and the topping is bubbling and golden.
9. Remove from oven and let rest for 10 minutes before serving.

TUNA PASTA BAKE

A quick and easy supper that can be thrown together with a few pantry staples. Quite simple to prepare and perfect for feeding unexpected guests. It's a budget friendly family meal that is a firm favourite with students and flatters.

Serves 4

½-1 batch garganelli or
    ditaloni (p.66)

420g can condensed tomato
    soup
1 cup soffritto
2 big handfuls flat leaf parsley
185g or 425g can tuna in oil
1 large tomato (optional)
½ cup cheese

Ingredient Note:
Instead of condensed tomato soup use a jar of pasta sauce/ puree or a 400g can of tomatoes, blended smooth and 2 T tomato paste thickened with a little maize cornflour.

1. Place a large pot of heavily salted water on to boil using a high heat.
2. Turn oven on to preheat to 180°C.
3. In an oven proof casserole dish on the stove top heat up the tomato soup, soffritto, chopped parsley and drained tuna.
4. When the pasta water is boiling rapidly, add the pasta, immediately stirring to separate. Boil uncovered until the pasta is very al dente (3 minutes).
5. Tip the drained pasta into the casserole dish and mix gently to coat with the sauce.
6. Top the dish with slices of tomato if using and sprinkle over the cheese.
7. Fan bake at 180°C for 25 minutes or until the cheese is bubbling and golden.

Variations:
Tasty additions to this dish are 4 big handfuls of chopped spinach and/or 1 small tin of sweet corn. Add these to sauce at step 3.

PASTA ALLA NORMA

This classic Sicilian dish from Catania in Sicily is said to be named after Vincenzo Bellini's famous 1831 opera lirica "*La Norma*". There is some debate about how the name came about but my favourite version is that the Italian writer Nino Martoglio, upon being presented with this colourful dish said: "this pasta is a Norma" (as the term Norma, after the opera, was at that time synonymous with perfection), and the name stuck. This dish relies on the perfect harmony of flavours between the four key ingredients - eggplant, tomatoes, basil and ricotta salata (ricotta that has been pressed, salted and dried). The result is simple, elegant and delicious.

Serves 4

1 batch garganelli (p.66)

4 T olive oil
1 onion (optional)
1 large eggplant/aubergine
Salt & pepper
1 clove garlic (optional)
400g can chopped tomatoes
1 T tomato paste
2 large handfuls fresh basil
Ricotta salata, cottage cheese or
 feta (to taste)

1. Dice the onion and eggplant into 1cm (½") cubes.
2. Heat the olive oil in a large frying pan over a medium heat, then add onion and eggplant stirring to cover all the pieces with oil, then seasoning generously with salt and pepper.
3. Put a lid on the frying pan and cook for 10 minutes stirring occasionally until the eggplant and onion are soft and browned all over.
4. Remove the lid and add crushed garlic, if using, and fry for a further 3 minutes.
5. To the frying pan, add the tomatoes and paste, mixing through, then let simmer gently until the sauce has thickened.
6. Meanwhile bring a large pot of heavily salted water to the boil using a high heat.
7. When the pasta water is boiling rapidly add the garganelli immediately stirring to separate. Boil uncovered until the pasta is al dente (3-4 minutes).
8. While the pasta is cooking, roughly chop the basil and add to the sauce, keeping aside a few leaves for a garnish.
9. Drain the pasta reserving a little of the cooking water.
10. Add the pasta to the sauce, gently stirring through until pasta is coated, adding in a little of the cooking water if needed to thin the sauce.
11. Serve, then crumble cheese over the dish and top with reserved basil leaves.

MACARONI CHEESE

The creamy, cheesy silkiness that is Macaroni Cheese (Mac & Cheese) is hard to beat, and a firm favourite with children and adults alike. Not an American invention as you might think, being first recorded in the 14th century medieval cookbooks *Liber de Coquina* and *The Forme of Cury*. Its availability as a packet mix has seen it become extremely popular with busy families, though it is so easy to make from scratch, and far tastier, that I do wonder why anyone would bother with a packet. Trust me and make this recipe at least once, I'm sure you will become a convert! It may not seem like this recipe makes enough for four but with a sauce this rich a little goes a surprisingly long way.

Serves 4

½ batch ditaloni (p.66)

4 T (50g) butter
4 T Pasta Blend (p.6)
4 cups milk
Salt & pepper (to taste)
3 cups cheese (grated)
1 cup extra tasty cheddar cheese (grated)
Paprika (optional)

Ingredient Note:
Use extra tasty or strong mature cheddar cheese to give the dish a delicious rich cheesy flavour.

1. Place a large pot of heavily salted water on to boil using a high heat. While it heats up make the sauce.
2. In a saucepan melt the butter over a low heat.
3. Add the Pasta Blend, and stir into the butter.
4. Remove from the heat and add the milk, bit by bit, stirring after each addition until well combined and the sauce is smooth.
5. Return to the low heat and stir until thickened, adding salt and pepper. The sauce should be very thick at this stage.
6. Remove from the heat and add the first measure of grated cheese, stirring into the sauce until melted and smooth. Set aside.
7. Turn oven on to grill (broil) setting.
8. When the pasta water is boiling rapidly add the ditaloni, immediately stirring to separate. Boil uncovered until the pasta is al dente (3 minutes).
9. Drain pasta well then mix through the cheese sauce.
10. Tip into oven safe serving dish(es) and sprinkle with the extra tasty cheese. Add a little paprika (if using) and grill (broil) until cheese is bubbling and golden brown.
11. Remove from oven and leave to cool slightly before serving. Enjoy!

Variations:
See the tasty recipes on the next page.

MACARONI CHEESE VARIATIONS

The options are almost endless as all sorts of ingredients can make a tasty addition to Mac & Cheese (p.73), even leftovers! Below are some of my favourite combinations to get your tastebuds tingling.

CRUMBED MAC & CHEESE: Mix 4 T of dried breadcrumbs, crushed cornflakes, potato chips or nacho chips with the cheese for the topping, sprinkle on, then grill (broil) as per the recipe.

MEATY MAC & CHEESE: Add your choice of ½ cup diced ham, cooked bacon bits, or prosciutto pieces to the cheese sauce.

CHICKEN & BROCCOLI: Dice 1 chicken breast and fry until cooked. Also cook 1 cup diced broccoli florets until just tender, drain well. Toss these with the cooked pasta before adding the cheese sauce. Or use leftover cooked diced chicken and broccoli.

SALAMI & PEAS: Cut salami into small pieces until you have ½ cup. Cook ½ cup frozen peas until just tender. Mix both ingredients with the cooked pasta before adding the cheese sauce.

CHORIZO & SPINACH: Slice the chorizo sausage into bite size pieces and cook through. Rinse 2 large handfuls of chopped fresh spinach then toss into the pan you used to fry the chorizo and allow to wilt for 1 minute. Take off the heat and add the cooked pasta and toss to coat the pasta in the chorizo flavoured oil. Then add the cheese sauce.

TUNA & BEANS: Drain a medium size can of tuna and break into flakes. Cook ½ cup frozen sliced beans until just tender. Mix both ingredients with the cooked pasta before adding the cheese sauce.

WALNUTS & BLUE CHEESE: Dice ¼ cup walnuts and 100g blue cheese. Add into the cheese sauce along with the cooked pasta.

THE HAWAIIAN: Add ½ cup diced ham and ½ cup well drained pineapple pieces to the cooked pasta. Then mix through the cheese sauce.

FOUR CHEESE: Add ½ cup each of diced camembert and blue cheese to the cooked pasta then mix through the cheese sauce topping with tasty cheddar cheese.

Some other yummy ingredients you could select from: caramelised onions, cauliflower, mushrooms, garlic, onions, capsicums, chilli peppers and spring onions. Fresh herbs like parsley and chives also complement the above variations.

MINESTRONE

It is actually quite tricky to write a recipe for minestrone as it is traditionally a "from the garden" soup that is made with whatever vegetables are in season. So now is the time to have a look in your vegetable crisper or garden and start creating your own traditional family recipe for minestrone! Below are some base ingredients to get you started.

Serves 4-6

½ batch ditaloni (p.66)

2 large handfuls flat leaf parsley
1 onion
50g pancetta or 3 rashers bacon
  (optional)
2-3 cloves garlic (crushed)
2 x 400g cans chopped tomatoes
1 bayleaf
4 cups diced vegetables: green
  beans, cabbage, zucchini,
  celery, leek, carrot, potatoes,
  spinach.
Salt & pepper (to taste)
1 can cannellini or borlotti
  beans (optional)

1. Dice the parsley and set aside.
2. Dice the onion and the bacon (if using) and fry in the soup pot along with the garlic.
3. Add the canned tomatoes, bayleaf and chopped vegetables. Cook for 10 minutes.
4. Add the ditaloni, beans (if using), chopped parsley, salt and pepper.
5. Cook until the pasta is al dente (4-5 minutes).
6. Serve with crusty bread and grated parmesan if desired.

Variation:
If you want to make this soup and your vegetable crisper bin is a bit bare add in 1 cup of soffritto with the canned tomatoes.

Cook's Tip:
If you prefer a thicker soup at step 4 crush some of the beans against the side of the pot with a fork and mix through the soup.

PASTA E FAGIOLI

This is a lightning fast soup to prepare if you have made the ditaloni ahead of time. This combination of pasta and beans creates a complete protein with all your essential amino acids. Hearty and filling this soup will keep away a winter's chill. The proportions are really only a guideline to get you started but note this is intended to be a very thick soup.

Serves 4-6

½ batch ditaloni (p.66)

2-3 cloves garlic
1-2 sprigs fresh rosemary
6 bacon rashers or 100g pancetta
2 cans cannellini beans
2 T tomato paste

Cracked pepper, olive oil & hot sauce to serve

Ingredient Note:
You can substitute 1-2 t bacon stock for the bacon if you wish, or leave out altogether for a vegetarian dish.

1. Finely dice the garlic and rosemary then set aside.
2. Dice the bacon and then fry in the soup pot until crispy. Remove half the bacon and set aside for a garnish. Add the garlic and rosemary and gently fry for 3 minutes.
3. Drain and rinse the cannellini beans then add to the pot, fry a little then add 1 can of water and the tomato paste.
4. Using a hand held blender roughly blend the soup (you still want some beans left whole) then add in the pasta and boil until the pasta is al dente.
5. Serve with the reserved bacon and cracked pepper sprinkled on top. Drizzle a little olive oil over the soup and let everyone add their own hot sauce to taste.

Variations:
Add 1 cup of soffritto along with the beans for an extra vegetable boost. Or soffritto can be used as a replacement for the rosemary and garlic.
Pasta e Ceci - substitute the cannellini beans for canned chickpeas and you have made a whole new dish!

SPECIALTY SHAPES

Specialty shapes are a lot of fun to make but it can take some practice to get consistent results and become fast at making them. Cavatelli, orecchiette and fusilli are best shaped on a wooden chopping board as the rough surface provides the texture you need to form the shapes properly.

CAVATELLI has two meanings in Italian but here we are talking about the shape that looks like little hotdog buns, though they also remind me of the commonly seen cowrie sea shells found all over the Pacific. A fun and easy shape to make that requires no special equipment, only a wooden chopping board and a medium size, flat bladed knife. Great for utilising in pasta bakes, with thick sauces and even in soups. You can make these any size you like by varying the size of the "sausage" you start with. I find the 1cm (⅓") size the most versatile.

To make: Pinch off a walnut sized piece of pasta dough. On a clean chopping board roll it into a "sausage" of about 1cm (⅓") thickness. Position the "sausage" at the top of the board with the length away from you. With a knife, cut approximately a ½cm (¼") off the end of the "sausage". In the same movement lift the knife and lie it almost flat on top of the cut pasta pulling the knife towards you with medium pressure. The dough should wrap around the knife ending up on the top side as you pull. It takes a while to get the pressure just right so if you have some that do not turn out as you would like, just gather them up and join back into the "sausage". Allow to dry for at least 30 minutes or overnight, on a clean tea towel.

ORECCHIETTE do look a lot like their meaning in Italian - "little ears" and come from Puglia in southern Italy. They are a bit fiddly to make at the start but a very versatile shape once you have mastered it. Use with chunky sauces, soups and salads. The larger version of this pasta, orecchio could even be stuffed.

To make: Follow the same method as for cavatelli. Once you have several cavatelli, take them one by one, gently unroll and turn inside out over your thumb or finger (depending on the size) pinching together the thinnest bit of the edge if need be to form an ear-like or bowl shape. This puts the rough side of the pasta on the outside of the shape, perfect for catching sauces. Allow to dry for at least 30 minutes or overnight on a clean tea towel before using in a recipe.

FARFALLE which means "butterflies" are more commonly known around the world as bows or bow ties. These also come in larger and smaller versions called farfalloni and farfalline respectively, and are often used in the cuisine of the Lombardy and Emilia-Romagna regions of Italy. Farfalle and farfalloni are seen in a variety of dishes often in multi-coloured combinations. The smallest, farfalline are usually reserved for soups.

To make: Roll out a sheet of pasta to 4 card thickness. Using a straight pastry wheel to cut the longest sides and a fluted pastry wheel to cut the shortest sides, measure and cut out the size of bows you want: 6cm x 4cm for farfalloni and either 5cm x 3cm (2" x 1") or 4cm x 2cm make nice sized farfalle. Use 3 card thickness for farfalline, and rectangles of 1.5cm x 1cm. Once the rectangles are cut, select one, and keeping it flat on the work surface use your thumb and forefinger to bring the edges together in a gathering, pinching motion. Like the other special shapes practice makes perfect and you will find that you can get quite fast at making these bows. Allow to dry for at least 30 minutes or overnight on a clean tea towel.

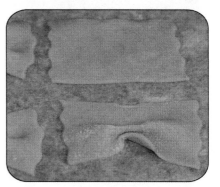

TROFIE from the Liguria region of Italy is a thin twisted pasta that is simple, quick to make and very filling. This is another shape that is great for keeping children occupied while you prepare the rest of the meal. Traditionally served with pesto sauces but can be used in pasta bakes too.

To make: Take pea sized pieces of the dough and roll between your fingers to make a tiny ridged sausage shape that is short with tapered ends around 2-3cm (1") long and about 4mm (¼") thick. You can make a thin sausage shape then twist it to be even more Trofie-like but that takes much longer and my quick version tastes just as good! It takes a while longer to cook than other pastas, up to 15 minutes, especially if it has dried a little.

FUSILLI are a very commonly seen dried pasta shape that look like a corkscrew and give great variety to any dish. These are really versatile if a bit tricky to make. The handmade version, unlike the dried pasta shape, is hollow inside and shaped more like a ringlet. Use with salads or any kind of pasta sauce.

To make: It can take a little time to master making fusilli but if you persevere you will be rewarded with a fantastically versatile pasta. You will need a wooden chopping board and a thin wooden bbq skewer. Using wooden tools is important to allow the pasta to grip and so enable the shape to be formed. Pinch off a marble sized ball of dough and roll into a thin sausage shape using the palm of your hand against the chopping board. The sausage needs to be about twice the thickness of the skewer and approximately 10cm (4") long. Let the sausage rest for a few minutes before shaping further. Place the pasta sausage diagonally on the board. Position the skewer across the board at the end of the sausage furthest away from you. The sausage should be touching the skewer at a 45 degree angle (making a slanted *T* like shape). Then lift the skewer onto the end of the sausage and pressing down lightly on either end of the skewer (not the middle) and keeping a steady pressure, begin to roll the skewer towards you wrapping the sausage around it, keeping your hands at either end. You can guide the sausage with your fingers as you roll to keep it at approximately a 45 degree angle to the skewer. Once you have the sausage completely around the skewer roll it gently back and forwards on the board a few times. Then carefully slide the fusilli off the skewer onto a waiting tea towel to dry. Let dry for at least an hour before cooking to ensure they retain their ringlet shape.

CAPPELLACCI DEI BRIGANTI – 'Brigands Hats' are pasta shaped like a pointy hat which is fun to make if not very practical. Great when used with a chunky sauce, though if you made extra large hats you could stuff them with a filling and then bake.

To make: Using a glass or circular cutter of whatever size you fancy, cut out the dough, and immediately shape into cappellacci.If you delay too long the edges of the circle will crack and not bend nicely. Wrap the circle around your forefinger and make a cone shape with the top third pressing down to seal the edges then take off your finger and bend up the edges of the circle to form the brim. Allow to dry for at least 2 hours or overnight on a clean tea towel.

FARFALLE WITH SAUSAGE IN A CREAMY TOMATO SAUCE

The type of sausages you choose to use in this dish will ultimately affect its flavour. I suggest something a little spicy, as it goes well with the sauce, though in that case you might want to cut back on the chilli - unless you like a dish hot. The addition of the cream gives this sauce a beautiful round taste as it mellows the acidity in the tomatoes. So in this case I think it is worth the few extra calories!

Serves 4

1 batch farfalle (p.81)

500g pork sausages (7-8)
1 medium onion (sliced)
3 cloves garlic (crushed)
¼-½ t chilli powder
400g can chopped tomatoes
1 T tomato puree
¼ cup cream
½ cup torn basil (optional)

Ingredient Note:
You can shape the sausage meat into mini meatballs or just break into pieces as you fry.

1. With wet hands, remove the cases from the sausages and put directly into a frying pan.
2. Cook the sausage meat on medium heat until it starts to release some fat then add in the sliced onion. Fry until everything is nicely browned.
3. Add in the garlic and chilli powder and fry for a further 3 minutes.
4. Add the tomatoes and puree, half fill the tomato can with water, swirl, and empty into the pan. Turn heat down so that the sauce only simmers.
5. Place a large pot of heavily salted water on to boil on a high heat.
6. When the pasta water is boiling rapidly, add the farfalle, immediately stirring to separate. Boil uncovered until the pasta is al dente (3-4 minutes).
7. While the pasta cooks, stir the cream and basil through the sauce. Drain the pasta reserving some of the cooking liquid.
8. Add the pasta to the sauce and mix through, this will finish cooking the pasta. Add a little pasta water if needed to thin the sauce so it coats the pasta evenly.
9. Serve. Buon appetito!

Cook's Tip:
The easiest way I have found to remove sausage casings is to slip a small sharp knife between the skin and the sausage so it splits along its length, then you can simply peel away the skin.

Variations:
Slice cooked cold sausages and fry in 1 T olive oil until nicely browned then proceed with the recipe as above.
Tossing in several handfuls of chopped fresh spinach at step 7 gives an added tasty vegetable boost to this dish.

TROFIE WITH MINT & PEA PESTO

Trofie, as well as being lots of fun to make, is really quick too. It is also a great pasta shape to get children involved in the kitchen, as they will enjoy rolling the tiny bits of pasta into "sausages". In fact, this whole recipe is so easy children can do it with a little supervision. It is a great way to get some vegetables into them too! Perfect for a quick, easy and healthy mid-week dinner.

Serves 6 as a light dinner

1 batch trofie (p.81)

4 cups peas (frozen or fresh)
16 large mint leaves (chopped)
4 cloves garlic (crushed)
1 lemon (juice & zest)
½ cup grated parmesan or extra tasty cheddar cheese
4 T olive oil
Salt & pepper (to taste)

Ingredient Note:
You can vary the quantities of any of the ingredients in this dish to suit your own taste.

1. Place a large pot of heavily salted water on to boil using a high heat. This is for the pasta.
2. Boil the peas in another pot for 3-5 minutes until just cooked. Drain and set aside.
3. Finely chop the mint leaves in a blender/whizz.
4. Add the peas, garlic, and most of the lemon zest reserving a little for serving. Process until a rough paste is achieved. Mix in the cheese then drizzle the lemon juice and olive oil until a nice consistency is reached. Season with salt and pepper.
5. When the pasta water is boiling rapidly add the trofie, immediately stirring to separate. Boil uncovered until the pasta is al dente (12-15 minutes).
6. Drain and put pasta into a serving bowl. Toss through the mint and pea pesto.
7. Serve with a little lemon zest and extra grated cheese on top.

Cook's Tip:
This pesto can also be made in a pestle and mortar or mashed by hand. It's nice to leave this pesto a little chunky rather than pureeing it but the choice is yours.

SMOKED SALMON FARFALLE

Flavoured pastas look wonderful in this simple dish. Try spinach, herb, carrot, capsicum, turmeric, tomato pastas or use a mix of several. If you want to make a more substantial lunch, increase the amount of pasta used.

Serves 4 as entrée or light lunch

½ batch farfalle (p.81)

1 T butter
1 clove garlic (crushed)
½ cup cream
Bunch of chives (chopped)
1 small lemon (juice & zest)
100g smoked salmon

1. Place a large pot of heavily salted water on to boil using a high heat.
2. In a small saucepan over low heat melt the butter then add the crushed garlic and fry for 2 minutes. Add the cream stirring to combine.
3. Add the lemon juice and zest (reserving a little zest to sprinkle on top). Mix well. Keep warm while pasta cooks.
4. When the pasta water is boiling rapidly, add the farfalle, immediately stirring to separate. Boil uncovered until the pasta is al dente (3-4 minutes).
5. While the pasta is cooking add the salmon to the cream sauce to warm up, breaking it into pieces as you add it. Stire in the chopped chives, reserving a little for a garnish.
6. Drain the pasta, then put in a serving bowl. Tip over the sauce and toss to mix through.
7. Garnish with lemon zest and chives then serve immediately with extra lemon wedges if desired.

Variations:
Dill makes a great substitute for the chives if you have it.
Cooked peas can also be added to the sauce for a vegetable boost.

SUPER SIMPLE SALADS

Here is my collection of go-to pasta salads that are easy to prepare yet look and taste delicious. Fantastic to use up that bit of extra pasta though they are all so tasty it is worth making pasta just so you can eat the salad. It is here where flavoured and coloured pasta really adds that extra something special.

All salads serve 4 as a main or 6-8 as a side

MANGO & MINT PASTA SALAD
Make the Mango & Mint Orecchiette (p.95) but leave out the peas. Serve cold on a bed of young cos or butter crunch lettuce leaves.

TUNA PASTA SALAD
Use a ½ batch squid ink pasta made into fusilli (p.82). Cook until al dente then toss in some of the oil from the tuna can. Serve with 185g canned tuna (in oil) and your choice of diced red onion, celery, baby corn, sweet corn, canned bean salad, sliced green beans and fresh flat leaf parsley.

MEDITERRANEAN PASTA SALAD
Use a ½ batch of pasta made into farfalline (p.81) cooked until al dente then tossed with either basil pesto or olive tapenade. Serve with your choice of diced green or black olives, cherry tomatoes, sundried tomatoes, feta, cucumber, anchovies, salami, celery, smoked chicken and basil. Squeeze over a little lemon juice and serve.

CREAMY PASTA SALAD
Use a ½ batch of pasta made into ditaloni (p.66) cooked until al dente. Cool and toss with a dressing made from ¼ cup mayonnaise and ¼ cup sour cream or Greek yoghurt, adding 1t horseradish cream or 2 t wholegrain mustard for extra flavour. Chop 4 hard boiled eggs into quarters, dice 4-6 rashers of cooked bacon and sprinkle over chopped spring onions or chives. Salami and gherkins are tasty too.

CHILLI & LIME PASTA SALAD
Use a ½ batch of pasta made into ditaloni, fusilli or farfalline cooked until al dente, then tossed in olive oil. Add the juice and zest of 2 limes and the following diced ingredients; 1 avocado, ½ red onion, 1 small chilli (seeds removed), ½ green or red capsicum, 2 cups cooked chicken, big handful coriander or flat leaf parsley.

BACON, BRIE & BEET LEAF PASTA SALAD
Use a ½ batch of pasta made into ditaloni (p.66) cooked until al dente and tossed with olive oil or your favourite vinaigrette. Add 1 small round of brie cut into pieces, 6 rashers of bacon (cooked and diced), 3-4 large handfuls of fresh baby beet leaves or spinach. Mix together and serve.

ROAST VEGETABLE PASTA SALAD
Use a ½ batch of pasta made into ditaloni, fusilli or farfalline cooked until al dente. Toss with a little olive oil and balsamic vinegar then add in several of the following roasted diced vegetables: eggplant, zucchini, capsicum, pumpkin, kumara, sweet potato and asparagus. Season with salt and pepper, freshly torn basil and crumble over feta if desired then serve.

HURRY CURRY PASTA SALAD
Cook 4 cups each of frozen mixed vegetables and pasta shapes until al dente, drain and cool. Warm together a dressing of ½ cup oil, 3 T lemon juice, 3 T peanut butter, 1 t curry powder. Mix well until combined into a sauce, then toss through the salad. Top salad with ½ cup roasted peanuts and serve.

PASTA ARRABIATA

This quick and simple dish of Roman origin translates literally as 'angry pasta' due to the addition of chillies. Just how 'angry' your pasta ends up will depend on you. Commonly served with spaghetti or penne, I think spinach cavatelli is just perfect with this sauce. I have also used soffritto, though not traditional, it adds great texture, flavour and nutrition to this sauce.

Serves 4

1 batch cavatelli (p.80)

1 cup soffritto
3-4 cloves garlic (crushed, if not in soffritto)
2 T olive oil
1-4 dried red or fresh chillies finely chopped (to taste)
Salt & pepper (to taste)
400g can chopped tomatoes
1 large handful flat leaf parsley

1. Place a large pot of heavily salted water on to boil using a high heat.
2. When the pasta water is boiling rapidly, add the cavatelli, immediately stirring to separate. Boil uncovered until the pasta is al dente (13-15 minutes).
3. In a large frying pan gently fry the chopped chillies, garlic and soffritto in olive oil.
4. Add the tomatoes, stir well and simmer until the sauce thickens. Taste test and add more chilli if needed then season with salt and pepper.
5. When pasta is done, drain then add to the pasta sauce along with the roughly chopped parsley. Stir and simmer for 2 minutes more.
6. Serve with parmesan if desired (though it is not traditional with this sauce).

POMEGRANATE & PESTO FARFALLE

Pomegranates add a jewel-like burst of colour to any dish. Here their juicy sweetness perfectly balances the saltiness of the olives and the oil in the pesto. Bursting with antioxidants from the pomegranates and iron from the spinach this stunning vegetarian dish is not only nutritious but surprisingly quick and easy to prepare. It is also excellent served cold as a pasta salad.

Serves 4 as main or 6-8 as starter

1 batch farfalle (p.81)

1 cup black olives
1 pomegranate (seeds)
Large bunch spinach
100g basil pesto

Ingredient Note:
In this recipe, fresh or frozen pomegranate seeds can be used. No need to defrost seeds before use.
Be careful when handling pomegranates as the juice can stain.

1. Place a large pot of heavily salted water on to boil using a high heat.
2. Rinse the spinach, shake excess water off and roughly chop any large leaves.
3. In a large frying pan or pot over a low heat wilt the spinach using the water that is clinging to it from rinsing.
4. Once wilted, remove from heat and add in the pesto to warm through.
5. When the pasta water is boiling rapidly add the farfalle, immediately stirring to separate. Boil uncovered until the pasta is al dente (4-5 minutes). Drain, reserving some of the cooking water.
6. Immediately add the pasta to the spinach and gently stir through the pesto until all the pasta is nicely coated, adding in a little of the reserved pasta water if needed to thin the sauce.
7. Toss in the olives and half of the pomegranate seeds. Mix through.
8. Transfer to a serving dish then sprinkle the remaining pomegranate seeds over the top.

Cook's Tip:
To deseed a pomegranate. With a sharp knife score around the pomegranate with just enough pressure to cut through the hard skin marking it into quarters. Break the pomegranate open with your hands. Place a quarter into a large bowl of water then using your fingers softly prize out all the seeds. They will sink to the bottom and the membrane will float which you can then skim off with a sieve. Repeat until all the seeds are removed. Drain seeds and lay on a paper towel to dry. As soon as they are dry, transfer to storage in an airtight bag or container either in the fridge for a few days or the freezer for up to a year.

CHOCOLATE FARFALLE WITH WALNUT CRUMBLE

A super quick dessert that is sure to please. I like to make extra of the nut crumble mixture and keep it in the cupboard so that when I need a dessert fix I can easily whip up this delectable dish.

Serves 6-8 for dessert

½ batch chocolate farfalle
  (p.21, 81)

¼ cup (40g) walnut pieces
2 T soft brown sugar
1½ t cinnamon
½ t mixed spice
¼ cup cream

Ingredient Note:
You can use other nuts such as almonds, hazelnuts or macadamias if you prefer.
The walnut crumble is also used in the Apple Ravioli recipe see p.108.

1. Place a large pot of heavily salted water on to boil using a high heat.
2. Dry roast the nuts in a hot frying pan, until they start to brown a little. Set aside a few larger pieces of walnut.
3. In a spice grinder or small blender process the remaining nuts until they are crumbs (not flour). Add in the brown sugar and spices and mix well.
4. Roughly chop the walnuts you had set aside then add to the crumble mix, this adds texture to the dish.
5. When the pasta water is boiling rapidly, add the farfalle, immediately stirring to separate. Boil uncovered until the pasta is al dente (3-4 minutes).
6. Warm the cream in a large saucepan then add the drained pasta and mix to coat evenly.
7. Serve the pasta then sprinkle the crumble mix on top.

Variations:
If you would like a chocolatey sauce, add 2 T of chocolate spread to the cream and mix until melted through and the cream has turned a beautiful chocolate colour.

MANGO AND MINT ORECCHIETTE

The mango brings a tropical twist to traditional pasta in this fantastic spring dish. A welcome change from the heavier sauces we tend to favour over winter.

Serves 4

1 batch orecchiette (p.80)

400g chicken breast (skin off)
2 rashers bacon (optional)
425g can sliced mango
1 large handful fresh mint
1 cup peas (fresh or frozen)
2 t maize cornflour
Salt & pepper (to taste)

1. Place a large pot of heavily salted water on to boil using a high heat.
2. Cut the chicken breast and bacon into bite size pieces then in a frying pan cook over a medium heat until golden brown.
3. While chicken is cooking remove 2 slices of mango from the can, dice and set aside.
4. Tip the rest of the mango including the canning liquid into a microwave proof jug, blend until smooth using a hand held blender. Cook on high for 1 minute.
5. Finely shred the mint, reserving a few small leaves for garnish. Add the mint to the mango sauce, stir through.
6. In a tiny bowl mix the cornflour with a little water to dissolve, then add to the sauce and stir through.
7. Once the chicken and bacon are nearly cooked add the peas and continue frying until cooked, then take the frying pan off the heat and set aside.
8. When the pasta water is boiling rapidly, add the orecchiette, immediately stirring to separate. Boil uncovered until the pasta is al dente (4-5 minutes).
9. Microwave the mango sauce again on high for 30 second intervals until thickened and hot.
10. Drain the pasta and put into the serving dish. Pour over the mango sauce. Add the chicken, bacon and peas, tossing gently to mix through.
11. Serve the pasta sprinkled with the diced mango, fresh mint leaves and seasoned with freshly ground salt and pepper.

FILLED PASTAS

There are 3 main types of filled pastas we will focus on in this cookbook and I have chosen the methods I think are easiest to follow for making each shape. However there are numerous techniques and shape variations for all of the filled pastas which you are welcome to try for yourself. The first filled pastas most likely came about as a smaller version of Torta, a medieval stuffed pie, commonly eaten in the Middle Ages in Italy. Each region, and often each town in Italy, has its own traditional fillings (and often a different name) for each filled pasta usually representing the common produce of the area.

I recommend you start making your filled pasta quite large and with 3 card thickness dough until you get used to the techniques. Then you can try making them smaller and with the thinner 2 card thickness dough. But as this pasta dough has no gluten and is therefore less stretchy when at only 2 card thickness, it can be quite tricky to successfully bend into shape without tearing. Ensuring your dough is a little damper rather than too dry also helps with bending and shaping.

I often like to make larger ravioli serving only 3-4 on a plate as an entrée or 2-3 for dessert which is very attractive.

Filled pastas can also be frozen. Leave to dry first, then free flow freeze on trays. After they are frozen transfer to a zip lock bag to avoid freezer burn. Best eaten within a month of freezing. Cook straight from frozen adding 1-2 minutes to the cooking time. Do not defrost before cooking.

MEZZELUNE (half moon) is a semi-circular filled pasta served with lighter sauces.

RAVIOLI is most commonly a square shaped filled pasta, though a round shape is sometimes used. Also served with lighter sauces.

To make mezzelune and round ravioli:

1. For both mezzelune and the round ravioli use a glass or circular cutter that is approximately 7-8cm (3″) across and has a fine edge which is better for cutting.

2. Divide the dough into egg size pieces and roll out into an oblong at 3 card thickness and as wide as your glass/cutter.

3. As each length is completed, cut out circles along the whole length then gather up the scraps and reroll. Keep the cut circles covered with a tea towel (dampened when really hot weather). It is easier to work with the pasta if it has dried out a little but not too dry as it will crack when you shape it. How long will vary with the weather but usually a few minutes is enough.

4. While the pasta rests, make the filling.

5. For ravioli take half the circles and place 1 teaspoon of filling on each one pressing it into a flat disc leaving about a ½cm (¼") around the edges. If unsure, start with less filling, as overfilling stuffed pasta is the fastest way to ruin it.

6. Using a little brush (or a finger) dipped in water, dampen the edges of the circles that have the filling. Then take a "lid circle" and place over the base and gently press down with the palm of your hand easing all the air bubbles out towards the edge.

7. For mezzelune put ½ teaspoon of filling off centre on all your circles.

8. Dampen the half of the circle that has the filling on it and fold over pressing out the air bubbles as for ravioli.

9. For both the shapes gently use fingertips to press around all the edges to make sure they are well sealed.

10. The ravioli and mezzelune are finished as they are, but to impress trim edges with a fluted pastry cutter, or cut again with a fluted scone cutter, or press with a fork.

11. Let the ravioli and mezzelune rest and dry a little for 15-30 minutes before cooking, turning over part way through so both sides dry evenly. This will help ensure that the filling will not leak out when cooking.

12. The ravioli and mezzelune can be made ahead of time. Once dry cover with plastic wrap and refrigerate until needed. If not using the same day, freeze.

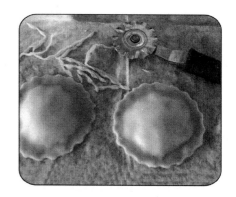

To make square ravioli:

1. Divide the dough into egg size pieces and roll each piece out into a 7cm wide oblong at 3 card thickness.

2. As each length is completed make sure you keep the dough covered with a tea towel (dampened when really hot weather).

3. While the pasta is resting make the filling.

4. It is easier to work with the ravioli if it has dried out a little but not too dry as it will crack when you shape it. How long will vary with the weather but usually a few minutes is enough.

5. Take one length of pasta and place a teaspoon of filling in the centre at 6cm (2¼") intervals, flattening the filling a little. Start with less filling as overfilling ravioli is the fastest way to ruin it.

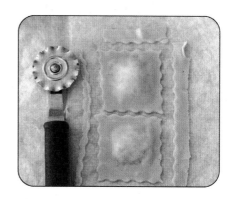

6. Then dip a finger in water (or use a little brush) and run it around the edges of the dough and between each filling.

7. Take another strip of dough and gently place it over the bottom strip enclosing the filling by gently pressing down on each filling with the palm of your hand and easing all the air bubbles out towards the edges.

8. Gently use fingertips to press around all the edges to make sure they are well sealed.

9. Repeat steps 5-8 for the remaining strips of pasta.

10. To cut to size, use a fluted pastry cutter and trim all the edges to 6cm (2¼") square ravioli. Gather up the offcuts and reroll them providing none have bits of the filling on them or are too dry.

11. Once cut to shape allow the ravioli to rest and dry a little for 15-30 minutes, turning over part way through so both sides dry evenly. This will help ensure that the filling will not leak out when cooking. You can also make the ravioli ahead of time. Once dry cover with plastic wrap and refrigerate if cooking later on the same day. If not using the same day, freeze.

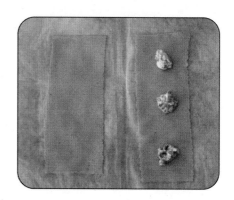

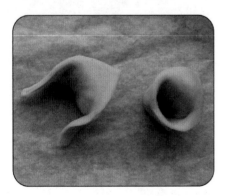

TORTELLINI (little pies) and tortelloni, which are larger, are made using either circular or square pieces of dough that are filled and folded then shaped into the traditional tortellini form. In Italy tortellini are usually served in a broth. There are other ways to make tortellini including starting with a circle of pasta but the method described below, I think, is easier to make and produces the nicest looking tortellini.

To make tortellini:

1. Roll the pasta out to 3 card thickness and cut into 5cm (2″) squares. Keep the squares you have cut covered with a dampened cloth until needed. If they dry they will crack when you fold them.

2. Imagine each square as two triangles. Put ¼ teaspoon of filling into the middle of one triangle. Then with a small brush or a finger take some water and wet the edges of the triangle with the filling on. If the dough is quite damp from the cloth you might not need the extra water to seal the edges.

3. Fold the empty triangle over the one with the filling on to totally enclose it making a little parcel.

4. Gently press all the air bubbles out towards the edges and press the edges together to seal.

5. With the filling side resting against a finger wrap the edges around the finger and press the ends together gently to seal.

6. Fold the pointy top of the triangle over rolling the edges down slightly too.

7. Repeat until all the filling is used up.

8. Place the prepared tortellini on a dry tea towel as you make them to rest a little before cooking. If not using soon after making they can be covered with plastic wrap and refrigerated, for a few hours, or freeze for later use.

PUMPKIN RAVIOLI WITH SAGE BROWN BUTTER

This is one of my favourite dishes to serve when entertaining as these ravioli are visually stunning and pack a flavour punch. If you really want to make a statement I suggest making the ravioli quite large and using two different coloured pasta doughs. Serve 1 or 2 of each colour per plate for an elegant starter or light meal.

Serves 8 as an entrée or light lunch

½ batch plain ravioli (p.98)
½ batch coloured ravioli (p.20)

For the filling:
1 cup pumpkin (mashed)
½ cup cream cheese
Grated nutmeg (to taste)
Salt & pepper (to taste)

For sage brown butter:
20 medium sage leaves
80g butter

Lemon juice & parmesan for garnish

A 7-8cm (3″) diameter drinking glass or a fluted cookie cutter

Ingredient Note:
To quickly cook the pumpkin; clean pumpkin skin, cut pumpkin into wedges, remove seeds. Microwave covered on high for about 5 or 6 minutes. Scrape flesh from skins and mash with a fork using a little butter or water to get the right consistency. It should be quite a firm but smooth mash. Dry fleshed pumpkin or squash work best with this pasta.

1. Prepare the dough circles for round ravioli.
2. While the pasta is resting, mix the pumpkin, cream cheese, nutmeg, salt and pepper together until well blended, and seasoned to taste.
3. Finish making the ravioli. While they rest place a large pot of heavily salted water on to boil using a high heat.
4. As the pot starts to boil begin the brown butter sauce by placing the butter in a frying pan over a medium heat. Watch it carefully as it will bubble, froth and then start to gradually turn brown. As it starts to brown add in the sage leaves to fry. This makes them deliciously crispy.
5. As the butter reaches a nice caramel brown, remove from the heat and it is ready to serve.
6. When the pasta water is boiling rapidly, add the ravioli one by one, gently stirring to keep separate. Boil uncovered until the pasta is al dente (4-6 minutes depending on thickness of pasta used).
7. Carefully remove cooked ravioli with a slotted spoon and leave in a colander to drain.
8. Plate ravioli up as desired, drizzle with sage brown butter and decorate with nasturtium flowers if you have them. Serve with lemon juice and parmesan for garnish.

Cook's Tip:
Making the sauce takes longer than you might think and should not be rushed or you risk burning the butter.

PESTO RAVIOLI IN SIMPLE TOMATO SAUCE

This is my adaptation of classic spinach and ricotta ravioli. Using cream cheese makes the filling easy to prepare and work with, perfect for the novice ravioli creator. Once you get the knack of making these larger ravioli you can easily adapt both their size and fillings to create many new dishes of your own.

Makes approx. 22 6cm ravioli

½ batch ravioli (p.99)

½ cup cream cheese
2 T basil pesto (drained)
400g can chopped tomatoes
Large handful basil
Salt & pepper (to taste)
Parmesan

Ingredient Note:
You can add more pesto to the filling if you like to suit your taste, just ensure that the mixture is still quite 'sticky', as too runny a filling is very hard to work with.
If you want to make smaller ravioli you will need to adjust the amount of filling per ravioli to suit the size.

1.   Prepare the dough strips for square ravioli, cover and leave to rest.
2.   While the pasta is resting mix the cream cheese and pesto together. Break up any lumps of cream cheese until all is thoroughly combined. Make sure to drain any excess oil from the pesto before using or it will leak out of the ravioli.
3.   Finish making the ravioli.
4.   Place a large pot of heavily salted water on to boil using a high heat.
5.   In another saucepan heat the tomato adding a generous handful of torn basil. Add salt and pepper. Leave to simmer and thicken.
6.   When the pasta water is boiling rapidly, add the ravioli one by one, gently stirring to keep separate. Boil uncovered until the pasta is al dente (4-6 minutes depending on thickness of pasta used).
7.   Carefully remove cooked ravioli with a slotted spoon and leave in a colander to drain.
8.   Serve with the tomato sauce, freshly grated parmesan and a few extra basil leaves.

Variations:
This is fantastic made with chunky 'pesto' style dips often found in the chiller section of the supermarket. I love using the roasted capsicum flavour. To use, replace the 2 T basil pesto with 2 T of the 'dip' of your choice. If using a strong flavour like capsicum the ravioli can be served without the tomato sauce, just a drizzle of olive oil, salt, pepper and freshly grated parmesan should suffice. Of course you can also use the more traditional finely chopped cooked spinach in place of the pesto.

TORTELLINI IN BRODO

This dish is traditionally served in central and northern Italy as an entrée on Christmas Day. But my super quick adaptation is simple enough to whip up on any chilly winter's day when you feel the need for a comforting broth. If you use tortellini from your freezer this dish can be on your table in under 10 minutes. How about that for impressing unexpected guests!

Serves 4

½ batch tortellini (p.100)

1 sausage (approx. 100g)
2 T parmesan or extra
   tasty cheddar cheese (grated)
1L gluten free beef broth/stock
Parmesan

Ingredient Note:
I use sausages in this recipe as the meat is easy to work with, making the recipe quicker. By varying the flavour of the sausage you can create a different dish every time. A time saving tip is to use readymade liquid beef broth/stock (or make it up from powdered stock) that way you can prepare this recipe quickly to feed a hungry family. If you prefer to make your own stock from scratch, recipes are easy to find.

1. First remove the sausage casing by slipping a small sharp knife between the skin and the sausage so it splits the skin along its length, then simply peel it away.
2. In a frying pan on a low heat cook the sausage meat, breaking it down as it cooks, being careful not to brown it as those bits will be hard to blend smooth and will make lumps in the tortellini.
3. In a mini blender/whizz process the meat while still warm along with the cooking juices and the cheese. Blend until smooth, almost like a paste. Put in refrigerator to cool.
4. Make the tortellini.
5. In a pot large enough to fit the tortellini put your broth on to boil on a medium high heat.
6. When the broth is boiling rapidly, gently add the tortellini, and cook until al dente (3 minutes). They float when almost ready.
7. Remove the tortellini from the broth and distribute evenly among the serving plates then pour the broth over the top.
8. Serve with extra freshly grated parmesan sprinkled over top.

Variations:
For an extra flavour boost, add to your ready prepared beef broth 1 cup of soffritto and blend until smooth.
Add an extra 1 tablespoon of fresh herbs to your filling; oregano or marjoram are nice, add to the blender at step 3 so they get chopped finely.

BLUE CHEESE TORTELLONI WITH BROCCOLI

A vibrant burst of colour and flavour are the signatures of this vegetarian dish. A few key ingredients are melded together to create a taste sensation.

Serves 4-6 as lunch

½ batch tortelloni (p.100)

For filling:
100g strong blue cheese
100g cream cheese

For broccoli puree:
1 head broccoli
2 cloves garlic (crushed)
2 handfuls fresh oregano
  or 1 T dried oregano
2 handfuls flat leaf parsley
Salt & pepper (to taste)
½ cup vegetable stock

Ingredient Note:
Depending on the strength of blue cheese used, if too much is added at step 3 it could be overpoweringly pungent in the finished dish.

1. Cook the broccoli in a steamer until very soft.
2. Meanwhile prepare the tortelloni using 6cm (2½″) squares.
3. For the filling the type of blue cheese used will determine the flavour intensity, so combine in proportions to taste by mixing the blue cheese with cream cheese until smooth.
4. Place a ½ teaspoon of the cheese mixture on each tortelloni then fold into shape. Allow 5–7 tortelloni per person for a lunch dish or 3 if serving as an entrée.
5. Set tortelloni aside to dry.
6. Place a large pot of heavily salted water on to boil using a high heat.
7. In a saucepan put the steamed broccoli and add all the other ingredients except the stock.
8. Use a hand held blender/whizz to puree until quite smooth adding in only as much vegetable stock as needed to make a puree consistency. Keep warm on a low heat until ready to serve.
9. When the pasta water is boiling rapidly, add the tortelloni one by one, gently stirring to keep separate. Boil uncovered until the pasta is al dente (4-5 minutes depending on thickness of pasta used).
10. To serve put the broccoli puree in the bottom of a bowl and lay the tortelloni on top. Drizzle over a little olive oil and grated parmesan if desired.

Cook's Tip:
If you would like to make the round tortelloni also shown in the picture use a 7cm (3″) circular cutter. Place filling on one half of the circle, dampen edges, fold over and shape by gently bending the edges around till they meet (see picture below).

APPLE RAVIOLI WITH CARAMEL SAUCE

This simple yet elegant dessert is the perfect way to end a meal. With 2-3 ravioli each it is just enough to leave you wanting more but not feeling like you have overeaten. Bellissimo!

Serves 4-6 for dessert

¼ batch ravioli (p.99)

For filling:
1 red apple
2 T cream cheese
1½ T walnut crumble (p.94
    finely blended, no nut pieces)

For caramel sauce:
½ cup brown sugar
4 T (50g) butter
1 T golden syrup
1 T maize cornflour
½ cup water
2 T cream (optional)

Ingredient Note:
In place of walnut crumble use
1T soft brown sugar, ¼ t cinnamon
and ⅛ t mixed spice.

Cook's Tip:
The apple filling can be made the
day before and kept refrigerated
until ready to use.

1. Over a saucepan grate the unpeeled apple. This ensures you retain all the juice and flavour from the apple.
2. In a small saucepan gently cook the grated apple over a medium heat until all the juice is gone and the apple is quite dry and starting to stick a little to the bottom of the pan. Take off the heat. Transfer to a bowl and leave to cool.
3. Prepare the dough stips for square ravioli and leave to rest.
4. Add the cream cheese and the walnut crumble to the grated apple stirring through to break up any lumps of cream cheese until thoroughly combined.
5. Finish making the ravioli.
6. Place a large pot of heavily salted water on to boil using a high heat.
7. Begin the caramel sauce by melting together the sugar and butter in a microwave proof jug on high for 30 seconds, or melt in a small saucepan.
8. In a small bowl make a thin paste by mixing 1 tablespoon of cornflour with ½ cup water.
9. Add to the buttery mixture and microwave again for 3 minutes, or cook stirring on medium high heat until the sauce becomes thick.
10. When the pasta water is boiling rapidly, add the ravioli one by one, gently stirring to keep separate. Boil uncovered until the pasta is al dente (4-6 minutes depending on thickness of pasta used).
11. Carefully remove cooked ravioli with a slotted spoon and leave in a colander to drain.
12. Plate up as desired and drizzle with caramel sauce. Stir the cream into the sauce just prior to serving (if using).

INDEX

Vanessa Hudson is the Gourmand Award winning author of the **Goodness Me it's Gluten Free** cookbook. A self-confessed foodie, she has travelled extensively exploring the culinary delights of six continents including many years spent in Europe where she fell in love with the Mediterranean way of eating. She has not let the need to eat gluten free compromise her ability to enjoy cuisine from around the world but instead has used that as inspiration for her latest cookbook **Goodness Me it's Gluten Free PASTA.** Vanessa began cooking at an early age, just as soon as she was able to stir a bowl and she has enjoyed putting her own spin on recipes, creating fantastic and imaginative food combinations for family and friends ever since.

Made in the USA
Monee, IL
23 September 2021